BEING
—IN THE—
BEING

The Person You Were Born to Be—
The Life You Were Born to Live

RAY CLARKE

PARTRIDGE

A Penguin Random House Company

To order additional copies of this book, contact
Toll Free 800 101 2657 (Singapore)
Toll Free 1 800 81 7340 (Malaysia)
orders.singapore@partridgepublishing.com

www.partridgepublishing.com/singapore

CONTENTS

To my wife Carolyn
Pure mind Pure heart Pure love Always

INTRODUCTION

Welcome to a new path on your journey of life, you and I are about to embark on a journey together, along the way you will contemplate various topics on life and behaviour that I raise, comparing the differences in our thoughts.

First, let me say that I have not achieved any professional degrees in matters dealing with the human being or any other beings.

I should mention that I grew up with a Christian background so any of my thoughts on religion, base from the knowledge I gained from that medium plus other material I have read, but it is not my intention to convert anyone's beliefs on religion or any other beliefs you have reached.

I will also mention that I have no experience or training in the skills of writing a book, like everyone else, I formed opinions about most things, which of course changed many times due to the various experiences and observations I have encountered during my life's journey to date.

For reasons I cannot explain, I felt compelled to put pen to paper to release my thoughts, which seem more cemented these days, even if it only enables me the opportunity to question those thoughts again.

I will say it had nothing to do with diets or exercise programs, although you will do no harm to your life path to be in balance with these items. Moreover, that regardless of age this concept is achievable, one, which I believe, enables you to be the person you were born to be.

This book is a tool for you the reader, when we reach the end of our journey together I am confident you will have learned three key areas for improving the person you currently are:

Firstly, you will have gained the knowledge necessary to identify life restricting behaviour patterns.

Secondly, you will have defined the areas to your current lifestyle behaviour patterns needing improvements.

Thirdly, you will know how to make the changes necessary for you to be living the life of the person you were born to be.

This book is also a journey in three parts:

In the first part of the book, I provide you with the information of the concept that convinced me that two intelligence systems control our behaviour patterns. I will provide you with explanations that define each system and helps you to understand how each one functions.

In the second part of this book, you will come to know the two intelligence systems that have directed you to the behaviour patterns you recognise as you.

You will recognise that your lifestyle and character are due to the behaviour of these two intelligence systems functioning within your body, which currently one system is more controlling over the other and any imbalance in your life is because of that control.

In the third part of the book, you will be able to clarify the areas where you need to improve the balance of the two systems for a better personal lifestyle. You also have the opportunity to perform the exercises that enable you to redirect your lifestyle to be the person you were born to be and follow the methods to pursue a career to do what you were born to do.

In order for me to provide my logic of thinking that led me to the concept of a self-reliant being in each being, it is necessary to start at the beginning of the thought train that led me through this journey.

Some of the topics may appear irrelevant to you through our journey, and at times, you may not agree with my thoughts as to how or why I came about my conclusions. That is what makes every individual unique, and to offer a challenge to the reasoning of any thought proposed by another human being is the sign of an enquiring mind.

You might feel inclined to skip parts of the book that include my thoughts and opinions, instead to delve straight into chapters that could help improve your life. However, you will miss important if not critical opportunities on personal observation assessment aspects of which you are now, how they developed and the changes needed. It may also be an insight to the impatience existing in your current behaviour patterns.

I am confident that by keeping an open mind until you complete reading the entire book and by participating in the activities, allows you to experiment with the opportunities evolving from your own thoughts.

The real bonus would be if you are able to expand on those thoughts to create an even better system for behavior than I am proposing, and you put it in writing to pass on to others, and that in doing so keeps improving humankind's life patterns.

First, I would like to explain to you my thoughts that led to this concept of two intelligent systems.

PART 1

CHAPTER 1

THE CONCEPT

Have you ever been waiting in line to be served in a store with the line three deep and only one sales assistant serving, and the thought enters your mind to just walk out with the product and not pay if the sales assistant does not hurry up. Then a second thought appears in your head telling you not to be so impatient the sales assistant is trying their best, that such an act will have you in court, so wait your turn.

Afterwards, you recall how you were so tempted to walk out but your conscience would not let you. How many times has this happened with all sorts of scenarios where one side of your thoughts are selfish, indulgent, criminal, etc. only to be scolded and overruled by your "conscience".

Two thought patterns constantly deciding your behaviour on how you should act, for some they will respond to the first type of thought in the above example. For the majority, the response of the second thought is the one they live by on most occasions.

This book is about those two thought patterns that are making you the person, you are today, and that the person you were born to be requires the equal involvement of both those behavioural thoughts.

What I am proposing is a concept of two intelligence systems currently co-existing within you as it does in all humans, that determines the person you become as an adult.

One form exists solely in the frontal lobes of the brain, as part of your persona, your creative and imaginative skills that I named as "Ego". The other resides in every cell of your being in the form of an "intelligence energy" that is responsible for your well-being and survival that I named as "Instinct".

In today's society, there appears to be a countless number of writers producing books, TV programs, documentaries, etc. attempting to help guide or lead people through their life. The choices seem to be endless whether its diets, religion, science, self-help, life styles, exercises, etc. the list goes on.

Ultimately who or what is responsible for guiding each and every "being" through the art of life, where referring to the term "being" for me includes the universe itself and each galaxy, solar system, star, planet, animal, plant, etc. right down to the single element necessary for the formation of this universe to exist.

I believe the truth is that somehow "something" does guide each "being" through its cycle of life from the moment of its conception, that all the required information that is necessary for enabling the survival of each "being" is included as part of the DNA at the point of conception.

What I am asking you to consider is that in every physical live "being" is an "intelligence energy" that is guiding that being through its life cycle and that all live beings have a life cycle.

For example, the "being" planet earth is at some point in its life cycle and the "inner being" or intelligence energy that is guiding planet earth is at some point. However, not necessarily at the same point, because once the planet has been through the lesson of death then the inner being in the beings task is complete and that intelligence energy will return to its origin.

In the case of planet earth, that origin is its solar system, but this now lifeless being will still be under the control of the intelligence energy of the solar system to enable the being that is the solar system to continue to function until its death. This one up path would be equally true for the cycle of the intelligence energy of any being that has ever existed.

Looking at the above example in the case of humans, the explanations in the following chapters will provide that life cycle detail. However at this point I am asking you to accept that humans also have in their DNA at conception the intelligence energy that provides them with all their functionalities, skills and talents to guide them through life.

With this in mind, in the lives of many people their lives have not been as fulfilling as other people are in their life, pondering those age-old questions and searching for the answers to understand the reason for their existence. Questions such as why am I here, what is my purpose in life, how does my life fit in, etc.

For some, those answers came to them at an early age and their life path has been quite clear, while for others it may take years and for some most of their life before the answer presents itself, if at all.

If you are waiting for, or depending on any form of outside help or guidance providing assistance to lead you through your life, then you could have a long and disappointing wait and find that when nearing the end of your time on earth to be still asking, "For what reason was I here".

I am here to tell you the answers to those questions have existed within you all this time but because you have been waiting for someone or something to provide the answers that you have missed, the opportunity to know what is possible. That in fact, the answers involve participation and achievements by no one other than you, that you possess all the skills necessary to ensure you achieve it, and that it is available to each of us.

For me, the concept that there is nothing controlling my life has ever been one that I have really contemplated, probably for the same reason as many other people, in that I do not feel that I am ever alone.

When I was younger whenever I would reflect on how my life was panning out to that point, I assumed that it had little to do with the decisions I had made. The idea of guardian angels guiding me seemed appropriate whenever I considered how fortunate I had been with the outcomes in my life.

However, once I recognised that even from an early age where I was the one responsible for the choice about any important directions my life had taken, providing there was a choice I was the one who had made that choice, and if I had to choose again, I would still make those same choices.

Many of the opportunities life has presented to me were not something I had specifically planned before the situation presented itself, and then my conscience selected it as the right choice to follow although my ego thoughts did not always agree as it had already made other plans.

I am suggesting here, there is a specific life path existing within you and one you should attempt to make a reality, especially if you are currently living in doubt about your life and peace of mind with any of the decisions made to date. Particularly those decisions that you made as your personal life choice that you feel is not providing you with the opportunity of being the person you would like to be, or living the life that you would like to live.

This will be a new life experience within the concept of your current lifestyle, without having to comprise any existing convictions and making your life that more interesting in the process. Once you start living the aims of the concept of the being in the being that I am proposing, I am confident you will see improvements and more contentment in many aspects of your life.

The first of my aims in this book is to assist you to understand the concepts that directed me on the path of the being in the being. The other is to assist you to recognise the possibility where redirecting your life will enable you to join me on that path.

I hope that this new path will be your preference once you have read my thoughts, which of course has now become my life preference because in reality we only live for a miniscule amount of time in the real scheme of things. That miniscule time is still your time and you can achieve the most fruitful life, a life that is available to each one of us, without causing interference or harm to this planet or any other being that exists on it while you are here.

My intention is to show that you and only you create that fruitful life through being the person you were born to be. Moreover, that it is the "intelligence systems" existing within you that is in fact the only true guidance factor available. The true-life path that will lead you in the right direction for any successful results you achieve in being that person during your lifetime.

Writing down the thoughts that you currently have on each of the topics, for comparison with your thoughts later in the book will assist to clarify if there is evidence of a need to redirect or adjust any of your current behaviour patterns.

CHAPTER 2

JOURNEY IN HUMAN BEHAVIOUR

B efore you can take the journey for tomorrow, you need to be aware of the journey responsible for which you are today. For who you are today was influenced by the acceptance of the behaviour by humankind to date that developed your behaviour and thought patterns, albeit unknowingly. As I moved into adulthood I tended to focus mostly on what life had to offer me, this all changed when my children came into my life and I felt it necessary to have the answers that provided them with every opportunity to become the best person they could be.

I began searching to understand what makes humans tick, why there are differences in people's behaviors and why some cannot achieve the ambitions they have for themselves. There had to be a connection between all beings that allowed them to behave as individuals while being a part of the whole, a common thread that was present for the entire life cycle of each being.

With that common thread idea in my mind, I decided to start at the beginning by reviewing human evolution concepts to help understand human behaviour development.

Defining how human behaviour evolved on the planet has involved scientific and theology experts who have provided different theories that with respect to science and religion will remain theories. For there is no way to prove either's theories and I want to make it clear that my aim is not to change any person's beliefs, ideas or convictions on such matters for they are your personal beliefs and no one has the right to change those ideals.

Religious explanations for the creation of the universe and humans in many races stemmed from a time when people knew little about the complexity of the universe or of life, and the non-existence of freedom of speech in those times meant people either accepted or forced to accept those religious explanations.

To maintain power over the masses the leaders of the lands outlawed doubting questions as evil, especially those doubting views of the leaders, claiming the perpetrators were possessed. This in itself affected the behavioural characteristics in humans afraid to question any of the principles of the laws set by their religious leaders. Thus, the behavioural mode became compliance by fear of death, forcing people's Instinct to focus mostly on survival allowing Egos' negative thoughts to flourish.

With the advent of education and the creation of democracy, for those believing religious concepts to be too simplistic, decided that the answers for the creation of the universe and humans lay in astronomy, the introduction of scientific reasoning led to the concept of the "big bang theory". This big bang created an infinite system with everything in balance and in control.

Religious followers found it difficult to accept the scientific reasoning for every "being" that has been created was due to the result of an unexplainable incident or accident.

Especially difficult to accept, was from that one incident or accident also enabled the creation of a planet with the conditions necessary for the biological miracle of life to occur. Living beings that required such intricate, interconnected systems to enable them to function, that humankind to this day does not completely comprehend resulting in humans evolving as planet earths' supreme individual?

Science theorised that each person had no connections to anything outside itself or guiding forces controlling their life. These theories enabled many people to turn away from the fear of religious repercussions creating a new direction for human behaviour patterns.

As part of science's theory concerning human evolution effecting whom we are today, Science want people to accept that human evolution originated via primates in Africa and then walked out to all parts of the planet.

Some questions remain without valid answers:

Why do those primate species that humans supposedly evolved from still exist in Africa? Why did they not evolve?

Did the ancestors of the primate species existing in many other countries that did not evolve into human beings also walk out of Africa?

Why is it that every other animal species was able to develop in the regions that they are in today?

How did the descendents of those that walked out of Africa once reaching their preferred region to reside in, develop specific skin colouring and facial features, different from the people that chose other regions?

To be fair, some religions also suggested that human beings originated from one source without explaining how the different races evolved.

For me, it seems a much more conceivable theory that primates and Homo sapiens have always existed as separate species. Moreover, that both species though similar in design had evolutionary paths of their own in the regions that each appears to have developed.

The question I ask is that because there are mountains with evidence of fossilized sea life indicating these mountains was once seabed. Thus, the seabed must once have been mountains. Therefore, is the best chance to discover information on human evolution by concentrating under the seas, not outer space?

Perhaps we could learn far more about ourselves if we found a way to search in that direction, rather than through the presumptuous ego controlled minds of humans theorising explanations for the formation of the universe or the creation of life, to me a task beyond the capacity of any human being regardless of their intelligence level.

There was another theory for those who refused to accept the ideas of human origins beginning on this planet, preferring to believe they were the descendants from another planet somewhere in the universe to support their belief in aliens. A supporting argument believing certain humans to be of another planet would be feasible to consider if we acknowledge there are people whose behaviors are alien to our instinct intelligence.

Since the keeping of records, there are those who have never been satisfied with other races living within their cultures and beliefs. Instead, greedily pillaged and plundered from country to country and savagely forced the people to accept the customs and beliefs of their attacker, often in the case of religion, beliefs stolen from a previously conquered race, and then claimed as their own.

In modern times, people responsible for the destruction of the rainforests, the pollution levels, the elimination of complete species of animals and plantation need to be included in this category.

Still, people need to make choices for answers to give them peace of mind, and people having deep convictions regarding any one of the above ideologies or any others for that matter will find it difficult if not impossible to alter their views and that is O.K. there is no need to alter those views.

Questions concerning the universe and life on the planet will probably be never ending, and science will continue to develop theories for study, and refuted by religious groups, you or I but realistically ever agreed.

To me we should look upon the continuous development of the human brain, as one of nature's mistakes. To this day, the ego intelligence level of the human brain continues to expand enabling them to increase their survival rates to levels resulting in populations reaching plague proportions.

The earth's capacity and/or human incapability to continue to provide the food supplies to sustain the existence of so many humans is now becoming apparent, that the environmental damage we are creating will greatly affect the ability to produce those quantities.

Humankind's current behaviour with greed for money and power over each other with little regard to date for the environmental results that are effecting and altering the planets' surface if allowed continuing, will certainly reduce and sadly in many cases eliminate many of the life forms that exist on this planet today.

To date there has been no acceptance of this mistake by the collective ego of humankind in fact for many they see all other animals and plants as provision for their existence to supply food, dwellings, clothing or entertainment.

A more urgent focus should be on the acceptance that we are restricted to this planet and that we do need to be directing our attention to resolving:

Firstly, the human plague developing on our planet today that will see the population probably triple over the next 100 years if left to continue its current course.

Secondly, how we will overcome managing the limited resources that are able to exist on the planet that will sustain all life, and not just for humans.

Thirdly, bringing under control the effects of climate change and pollution overall that is destroying the planet's resources that sustain life.

If we continue on our present course, "Nature" or "God" will have to step in and bring things back under control as apparently occurred with the end of the dinosaur age after a meteor directed to this planet. Because the reality is, just like dinosaurs, human beings are not essential to the well being of this planet or the universe.

Geologists tell us that there have been four periods of ice ages on this planet to date, which is a form of control available to the planet to restore any imbalance on its surface. Just as any type of plague to reduce excessive numbers of plant or animal requires production by the planet and equally for the destruction of that plague as another part of its control systems to maintain balance.

The reality is it will probably be the functions of human behaviour rather than any universal or planetary behavior that will significantly alter the way life on this planet will function.

Nonetheless, to me for countries spending vast amounts of money trying to conquer outer space is a waste and futile. Because the reality is, that it will not change anything that is occurring to planet earth today or improve the current attitude of humankind behaviour.

It would be difficult to move away from any beliefs you have in your life, beliefs that you may have held since childhood, most likely indoctrinated by your family circle. You certainly cannot change what has occurred in the past with regard to the treatment of other cultures, or the extinction of other animal and plant species due to human greed.

Those behaviours and theories of our ancestors created the society that exists today influencing the behavioral thoughts and patterns that helped make you the person you are today. The unfortunate outcome resulted in what I have termed an ego-controlled mind for the majority of humans.

You do have the opportunity to improve personally the way you live today via the choice of including the concept of the being in the being in to your life. A concept that may provide the opportunity for you to influence others to accept and eventually one by one will help change human behaviour.

This ego-controlled influence of society today will make it difficult for you to make any changes to your life style, especially your behavioural mannerisms. That is the challenge I am asking you to take with this book and one that must be yours alone.

The reason I say this is that no two people have the exact behavioural patterns provided to them on conception, that is what makes us individuals and that is why you should not involve anyone else in determining the person you were born to be.

Although my journey in human behavior did not provide me with complete or valid answers, I did conclude that science went the road of the ego intelligence as the accepted means for behaviour and thinking as instinct intelligence was too abstract. Though religious concepts originally followed the instinct intelligence path that guided humans to a more civilised culture, it too now for the most part follows the ego intelligence behaviour.

However, this part of the journey did lead me to the concept of the being in the being, the common thread that exists in all humans and all other beings that started my search on behaviour. The thread that has enabled the survival of all live beings and I believe it exists in the form of an intelligence energy which I hope to clarify for you over the following chapters.

CHAPTER 3

DEFINING INTELLIGENCE ENERGIES

Through the remainder of Part 1 I will provide the explanations and reasoning's that led me through this path, which assist you to become familiar with the different forms of intelligence I believe exist that is controlling yours and my behaviour.

To explain that common thread I refer to as intelligence energy, it will be advantageous for you and for me to put some readily accepted, well-hackneyed names to tag the intelligence energies I will be discussing to help reduce any confusion as to which "being" I am referring.

The name to define the intelligence energy system in the "being" known as the universe that ensures each being in the universe is performing exactly as it should to maintain the perfect balance of the universe; I shall refer to as "God" however it is not to be meant as an implication to any religious deity.

It would of course be necessary for this "inner being" known as "God" to exist in each being in the universe in order for them to function in conjunction with the universe.

Therefore, at the point of conception of all beings that intelligence energy must for part of what can be termed as the DNA of any being.

For our purposes to reduce confusion and repetition when referring to the term god, it will include the intelligence energies of our solar system and galaxy, which in reality have their separate intelligence energy that also play a part in the life of planet earth.

In the case of planet earth, the name to define its intelligence energy that has the combined intelligence energy of the universe and a planetary intelligence energy that ensures the planet is functioning, as it should, I shall refer to as "Nature." The function of this inner being called "Nature" is quite different to the universal inner being called "God" that is why god does have to be present in nature.

The being that is the planet will still need to spin on its axis and hurtle through space at thousands of kms/hr. on an exact journey around the sun, long after it becomes a "dead planet". This is because the intelligence energy that is guiding the solar system also exists in the being that is planet earth, as well as the other planets in its system.

If this energy dissipated when the planet died, would allow the dead planet to drift off into space destroying the balance of the solar system and possibly destroy the balance of the galaxy. If which was possible would have certainly resulted in the universe's demise long ago if there were no controlling factor (god) in place for every "being" existing in space.

The inner being I named as "nature" primarily is to guide the planet through its life cycle where god provided the information into the DNA of planet earth at its conception that god gathered when involved in the creation and death of other planets in the universe.

Therefore, volcanoes erupt when they are supposed to, earthquakes occur where there required to, earth's temperatures and pressures are controlled, water is present in the right places, the ozone layer protects the planet's surface and so on. In addition, while only god determines the end of life for planet earth, nature, under the guidance of god, does have the capacity to alter or end, any or all life forms that exists on the planet's surface.

Acceptance of this concept of a being in a being leads us in the direction that any form of being, plant or animal, that exists or has existed on this planet. At its point of conception, into its DNA be implanted the combination of universal intelligence energy (god) for it to function under the universe's conditions, planetary intelligence energy (nature) for it to function under the planets conditions.

In addition, a species intelligence energy specifically for that category of being, needed to assist in guiding that being through its life cycle on the surface of the planet.

The name for this inner being of combined intelligence energies I refer to as "Instinct" and it can be witnessed at any moment, on any position on the planet, by any plant or animal existing at that moment and it is their true "being in the being."

Whether it is plant or animal the elements and energy needed to create each being, requires determining by god and nature to ensure the balance of the planet's resources, as those resources provided the ingredients that created every "being" existing or that existed on this planet.

Somehow, the miracle of life allowed elements to unite forming cells, which in turn those cells united, creating a new level of intelligence for the newly formed cells. And so over the eons on planet earth began the production of intelligent beings ultimately in the form of plants and animals, all containing the level of a combined intelligence energy in every cell of their being to guide that being through its cycle of life.

As each being evolved, the different requirements of instinct were created for the survival of that being, therefore each form of plant life has its own intelligence energy just as does each animal.

This intelligence energy in every being is dynamic, for at any given moment when implanting "instinct" into a new beings DNA it also has to include the knowledge for surviving that the instinct of that being has gained to date. In addition, in every animal produced, within the instinct required for their life cycle will also include their behaviour patterns.

There have been many studies on the subject of instinct, regarded by many, especially with reference to plants and animals in their natural environment, as all being a part of "nature". Yet the instinct behavior of any plant or animal is precisely the way they should be behaving. Which in the context of these two energies that I am referring to, although interconnected have very different functions on an intelligence level?

As animal life evolved, they developed another level of intelligence that works in conjunction with instinct. This is the point where plant life and animal life differentiated, as most forms of animal life continued to evolve developing a second intelligence to increase the opportunity for their species to survive.

A system I best describe as the support intelligence system that developed in the brain through the need of an environment awareness system for each species when their mobility increased. The system that I refer to as "Ego" is present and involved to various degrees in every species of animal life existing on the planet. Moreover, how it effects and controls the life of every human is the core reason for this book that we will discuss in detail in later chapters.

This journey from a single element of planet earth into beings having the combined capacity of four intelligence systems has taken billions of years to evolve, and just like our questions of the universe, the answers to the many questions of that journey are most unlikely to be forthcoming.

CHAPTER 4

UNDERSTANDING THE INTELLIGENCE ENERGY

I have a theory I would like you to consider, providing you have accepted the concept of intelligence energy, on what happens to those energies when the body dies.

Einstein's theory states "Energy can neither be created nor destroyed" If correct, then this combined energy I call instinct must still exist on this planet, no matter how miniscule, containing or sharing the instinct knowledge gathered from the experiences learned by that being.

I am not suggesting any religious connotation here because the body, which includes the brain for all animals, is no more upon death and the persona that existed in that body dies with it. Still, I believe that the intelligence learnt by the energy system used to support that life passes over to the larger intelligence energy systems of nature and god for any future beings instinct.

This continual updating of the intelligence energy system then used to assist next generation animals and plants alike to cope with the ever-changing characteristics of their species on this planet. Indicates to me that the more we can focus on those energies as a way of improving life for ourselves that in death, all is not lost, instead we have served one of the purposes we were born for, enabling life to continue in a more positive manner.

Of course, this is but another theory, and yes, one by a nonprofessional. One, I view as a combination of science and religious theories that provides hope for my ego that life has more than one existence, even if it is no more than energy it once was my intelligence energy.

Another theory I have for you to consider is the possibility that the religious masters who achieved the level of attainment to their "universal energy" that spoke of life after death were referring to this scenario of our intelligence energies returning to their origins, specifically the pure love existing in our instinct returning to the universal energy.

Therefore, when pure love exists in any being, then in their death that love returns as part of the universal energy in nature, if this is extended to all facets of the energies in instinct then this would allow the energy cycle to remain in balance.

This theory opens the possibility that the religious masters who experienced this phenomenon would have had little difficulty in claiming the existence of a life after death that was far superior to any they had known on earth, which they named as heaven.

Neither theory of mine will have any impact on you achieving your goal to become the person you were born to be or the life you were born to live. I will point out references throughout the book, which I believe provides substance to consider.

It is necessary for you to understand how I perceive each of the four intelligence systems exist in relation to human beings. The misconceptions by many humans today, are that they have to find their truth "out there" that humans are separate from other beings on the planet.

In my opinion, it is actually the opposite, for as I stated whether it is plant or animal the requirements for the creation of each is from the elements of this planet, and each have acquired the necessary intelligence energy needed for their survival from the planet as well, which in reality connects us to all things.

There is also the need to realise that on a day-to-day basis today for most humans, there is awareness of only one intelligence system, which is due to our acceptance of this once the ego develops control of day-to-day thoughts, inhibiting our ability to experience these intelligence energies.

Equally important then, is for you to make your ego aware the intelligence energies that make up your instinct are present within you to ensure your very existence. Moreover, are functioning independently and in unison as required for your entire life cycle, equally for that of every animal and plant.

This next step in your journey is my definition for each of the intelligence systems to give you a better understanding of how I view each, and to observe my understanding of how their roles interact.

At the same time, I will provide the methods possible for experiencing these intelligence energies that will help to enable seeing your true self and achieving this is by searching within yourself to where each exists through the aid of meditation.

1. EGO

There was a time back at a point in evolution when all life depended entirely on instinct to survive. This all changed with the development of a support intelligence system within the brain of the animal world, and I believe its original function was designed for storing the information received from the senses for analysis by instinct.

As the animal world became more mobile and needing an immediate knowledge of the territory to escape the dangers that existed. Ego developed into a short-term memory support to enable each animal to familiarise itself with its habitat. This development increased the ability of ego to assist in surviving in innovative ways, competing against the natural hazards of nature, against other species for food and against predators.

The direction of a life as an omnivore provided prehistoric humans with the opportunity to consume more of the earth's elements than any other species, enabling the continued expansion of the ego area of the brain by absorbing much of those new elements consumed. Thus increasing the ability to learn and retain more of both the instinct and ego type knowledge-expanding capabilities.

As humankind continued to develop, this retention capacity pushed humankind above all other animals in the intelligence level. So much so, that since humans have reached the point to what we term as modern man, the ego intelligence in the brain has the ability to develop so quickly from birth that it believes its section of the brain is not only the integral part for which it is responsible but also controls the entire brain.

In reality, the ego intelligence does not commence functioning until after our first breath. Imagine the trauma during the pregnancy and birth if the ego-based fear was in control of the fetus during that period, the death toll for mother and baby would be catastrophic.

Therefore, the body relies entirely on instinct to survive during birth and those critical early weeks of life, while ego is content to play the role of observer, absorbing and processing all the information of its surroundings, people and its body.

The learning phase develops rapidly, so much so that within 3-5 years it is in control of the day-to-day thoughts, though with little rational. Moreover, experts now belief this intelligence does not fully develop until our 25th year of life.

Unfortunately for many, also believing it alone controls the whole body and every function that its body performs, and in general no longer accepts the importance of, or for the majority, the existence of any other form of intelligence. This non-recognition leads to distorted views by ego of instincts guidance, nature's spirituality and gods pure love, which all form the very essence of our being, these distorted views we will look at in detail in later chapters.

However, at this point it is important to recognise that the original creation of the ego was purely to deal with the peripheral circumstances in the lives of all animals. That in humans when allowed having complete control over thought patterns has a tendency to over focus on the self.

Unfortunately, those thoughts can result in existing at either end of the extreme whether positive or negative. Typically, in such areas as self-absorption, self-praise self-abuse, material possessions, etc. in many instances with little regard for the wellbeing of any other being on this planet.

Accepting that ego does not mature until we are 25 years old, equally to consider dementure of the ego may commence by the time we are 55 years old. Then for some, the ego area of the brain will only operate at its peak for 30 years if all goes well. If this is true then each of us are dependent on instinct more for the greater period of a normal life span and need to be more accepting to instincts thoughts.

It is also important to be aware that the ego is extremely essential to the overall well-being of humans on a daily basis, playing a significant role in our life cycle, personality traits and our imagination. Ego creates the fun in our life enabling our participating in activities the instinct would not allow us to do if it had complete control, especially anything instinct viewed as dangerous to our health, well-being or existence.

Ego is always present in our thoughts when it is not sleeping, if used correctly in the manner designed for, ego can and will continue to help improve our lifestyles.

2. INSTINCT

The greatest gift to any living being on earth, whether it is plant or animal, is that of instinct, and none more so than it does in humans, existing in every cell in your body. Instinct enables you to survive as a complete being, and this occurs in each live being on this planet.

At the instance conception is achieved, the establishment of the DNA strands and genes necessary for creating a unique being is completed by implanting the latest version of instinct to those strands and genes enabling life's miracle to commence.

The instinct begins its guiding role from day one of conception, involved in all internal and external body development, individual organ functional operation, muscular development, nutrition distribution, etc. and the coordination of all bodily functions necessary for the body to survive as a lone entity for its life cycle.

Each cell in the human body has the capacity to operate separately or simultaneously with every other cell in the body. To add to all this wonderment the continuous replacement of every cell in the body is necessary to keep each part in maximum health until the completion of the body's life cycle.

All is a requirement for instinct to know and control including how to be born continuing after birth in your growth and survival, guiding you through your life cycle and through your death cycle as the "true being in the being".

Acceptance that this intelligence energy exists in every cell in your body and that it exists in every other "being" living on this planet to ensure that being is functioning exactly as it should.

Then instinct must condition the ego to realise that it is not actually in total control of anything more than its own thoughts. Nor should you allow the ego to try to block the opportunity for you to be able to use this intelligence, which is readily available to each human being. For once the random thoughts of the ego can be calmed the thoughts of your instinct will be present.

Instinct exists on another level, generally referred to by the term as the "inner self" or "conscience", which is the intelligence you are experiencing whenever those opposing thoughts in your head are in a conversation trying to calm or manage the often-overzealous random thoughts of suggestions, judgments, plans or schemes of the ego.

These conversations can also take the form of electrical impulses or chemical releases from other organs in the body such as the stomach, skin, Heart, etc. whenever the ego's thoughts become irrational or the senses inform the possibility of a danger to the survival of the body.

It is also in this area of the inner self that you have the greatest opportunity to understand humankind's existence. For as stated earlier, all the knowledge humans have gained for their survival to date is stored in a separate area of the brain to ego. Generally referred, as the "sub conscience" which is that part of the brain where all the knowledge of your instincts behavior patterns and body organ communications performed exist.

You need to be mindful that ego also has access to that stored information in your sub conscience and recognises that it would have far less control over your thoughts if it allowed instinct to be readily accessible.

Therefore, ego will make every effort to dominate and control your thoughts, specifically with the intention to divert any thoughts arising from your instinct. Especially when it is aware, that instinct is the more passive intelligence, allowing ego to dominate if persistent enough.

3. NATURE

This intelligence energy exists more specifically in the planet itself but also in every cell in your body and equally in every other "being" existing on this planet. Its functions are:

Firstly, to ensure that the planet is functioning exactly as it should, which we discussed earlier.

Secondly, to ensure any beings existing on its surface are not suppressing that function,

Thirdly, to provide the intelligence necessary for any beings created on the planet that will aid in their survival from the gravitational forces, the rays from the sun, gases, etc. that keeping the planet alive produces.

You need to allow both the ego and instinct to realise that at that level neither are in control of anything other than their own thoughts. Nor allow them to deny your body the opportunity to try to experience this intelligence energy.

This is attainable for all of us usually through the practice of one of the many forms of meditation or prayer. For once the ego is calmed of its random thinking and then the instinctive thoughts have also been quietened, your body is able to experience nature's intelligence energy existing within it.

At this level, there is no communication but a feeling of a different form of belonging than that experienced between humans. Because as mentioned, due to every element of our being is derived from the planet as is the elements of every other being around us, it is quite easy at this level to feel you are not just a part of the animal kingdom but also the mountain, ocean, trees or even your own backyard garden.

When you are at this particular level there is also a knowing that it is a greater intelligence, often referred to as "spiritual awareness" because you realise it is more than your body or your mind and that at the end of your life cycle all the elements of your body's cells will return to the planet.

Yet, there is a part of you that is more than the physical elements of the planet very often referred to as your "soul," nature's intelligence energy existing in your body, and like the elements in your body will return to its origin, that origin being nature.

4. GOD

Acceptance that this intelligence energy exists in every cell in your body and that it exists in every "being" in the universe and that its function is:

Firstly, is to ensure all beings are functioning in conjunction to keep the universe in balance.

Secondly, that each is also functioning exactly for the purpose they were created.

Thirdly, that it is providing the intelligence energy necessary to enable each being to withstand the forces the universe produces.

You must realise that this is the infinite intelligence, and that it has ultimate control over all beings. In addition, it requires the need to still the other three intelligence types in order to provide you even the opportunity to experience this energy.

Which I believe is remotely possible to attain, mainly through the skills achieved in the process of extensive and intensive meditation through total submission of the self to rise above natures' intelligence until reaching the point when the universal intelligence energy in your being is present.

This is one area that it will not be possible to experience unless many continuous hours, often years, are spent remaining in total solitude and in deep meditation (Moses on the mountain top, Jesus in the desert, etc.) and even then it may elude you. Those that do attain it are afterwards often highly spiritually motivated people that we recognise as spiritual masters and in some cases either have been, or still are, revered even worshipped in various cultures of humankind.

At this level, none of humankind or nature's physical senses is present, yet there is still this intuitive knowing that something greater than life as we know it exists here, often referred to as "pure love" which is in fact the universal intelligence energy. In addition, it is beyond the realm of the existence of sound, colour and light just a knowing that this is the true place of origin of the intelligence energy for all beings and that everything is, as is meant to be.

For the overwhelming majority of humans the only experience with this energy will come in the form of pure love. That love I will discuss in more detail shortly, however for now the realisation should be that the Instinct contains this energy plus two others to help guide you through your life that Ego pretends does not exist unless it suits.

PART 2

TWO THOUGHT PATTERNS

For the most part your ego is in control of your thoughts and activities on a daily basis in today's society, deciding what you eat, how to spend your time, with whom to spend your time, your relaxation and fun times, and many more.

Sadly, for many people they also allow ego to control their behaviour patterns, it is important to accept that a balanced behaviour for any human being is not achievable just on ego intelligence; you need the input of your instinct intelligence to provide guidance, particularly for the dominant ego attitudes in many of today's human.

It is also important to be aware that the design of your body and mind is for instinct and ego to function as a united team finalising any important life decisions with equal inputs of thought and equal agreement on any outputs if your life cycle is to reach its full potential.

Through instinct, you can attain the highest level of achievement that your body and mind is capable of achieving. It is also necessary to be aware that beyond survival, instinct is just as content to settle at any level of achievement that the ego is prepared to settle.

Unless the instinct is inspired and encouraged to reach higher levels of achievement by the ego, the body will not reach those upper limits, because only instinct can create the conditions required for your body and mind to perform to your maximum potential, ego can only create the desire.

In order to understand the two-intelligence systems better I will now need to describe in more detail the function of each, what each has the capabilities of performing, and how each one interacts with the other.

CHAPTER 5

INSTINCT CHARACTERISTICS

To elaborate on statements made earlier, when ego begins learning each task performed by its organs and general body capabilities; it also commences to form its own personality.

Falsely assuming that it is the one controlling all the tasks and knowledge, assuming also that as the owner of the body has total responsibility as the being in the being.

In my opinion, humankind through the discovery of organ transplants has supplied proof why this concept of ownership is false. For example, when it is determined that a body is medically "brain dead" i.e. deeming neither the ego intelligence nor the instinct intelligence to be functioning in the brain organ.

That by placing the brain damaged body on a machine designed to keeping that body "alive," the remaining parts of the body will continue functioning until the organs or any other healthy parts of that body required, are then removed and placed into a second body, where those same organs or parts previously owned by the second body failed.

Those transplanted organs or parts will then continue with the aid of the instinct intelligence in the second body to function in conjunction with all of the existing organs of that body, including the ego of the second body.

Importantly, now two different intelligence systems than was previously operating those transplanted organs or body parts. This in my mind demonstrates that each part of our body has its own instinct intelligence system, and that each is dependant only on being a part of the complete body.

The question I ask is if it is possible that because human instinct intelligence is all from the same source (per my theory) makes it feasible for the parts of different bodies to accept and function in other bodies.

That it is especially wrong for us to still assume we have ownership of our bodies upon our death, that still have all those wonderful parts that are sometimes quite healthy and able to be used to improve the life of many ailing people on this planet through a system of a compulsory worldwide donor program.

Examples of the above need reminded to ego every time it starts to claim superiority over the instinct for it will and the only way to keep ego grounded is by highlighting instinct features.

It is also possible to observe unique behaviour patterns in animal and plant species or varying degree of these Patterns where the ego intelligence maybe considered as minimal or nonexistent that will raise the profile of instinct.

Common examples to observe are; trees that drop their leaves when rainfall is low, flowers that close their petals when the sun has set, animals in paddocks move away from trees during an electrical storm.

There are many examples and writing a book for each being may be possible. Therefore, it is disappointing that with our advanced ego intelligence; we have failed to develop our capabilities in all areas of the instinct, or realistically, rediscovered it to our advantage.

To understand the unique characteristics of the instinct better, it will require me to provide more detail into the makeup of the instinct. In particular, the area of the senses, especially the existence of a sixth sense I called emotive, the genes and the issues you will need to overcome to raise the profile of your instinct.

THE SIXTH SENSE

The degree of independence for any animal to survive is the gift of the senses, and I believe human beings fall in the category of animal genetically having the capability of "six" The five physical senses—sight, smell, touch, hearing, taste and a sixth I will call "emotive".

The design of your body is such that each sense has the capacity to act independently or simultaneously with the other at any time and with every cell in your body thus enabling the many terms of reference such as Goosebumps, lump in the throat, knot in the stomach, the list goes on.

The acceptance that you have six senses and that each is a part of your instinct and not your ego is not easy, as I said the ego views itself as the supreme entity of the body. However, if you consider that throughout the animal chain (which includes humans), one or more of those senses exist in all animals and is accepted as being essential for its survival.

Much is already in writing about the existence or non-existence of a sixth sense, disregarded by the ego; which it identifies as false claims of people and animals having the ability to foretell the future. Ego considers it an abstract condition, which does not fit into any physical criteria that is receivable by its accepted five senses that assist it in your survival and at an early age convinced itself that it alone is responsible for you.

In my opinion, the emotive sense is in fact instincts main sense and is communicating with every cell in your body at all times, that your reactions to the information provided by your body including the five physical senses is guided by the response from your emotive sense.

A common example for many people is when looking over a balcony on a high building; the ego thinks there is nothing to fear because there is a railing. Nonetheless, the eyes view the distance to the ground, the emotive sense responds to the signal as dangerous, and the adrenalin begins to flow, then the body becomes uncomfortable especially in the stomach and legs.

Similarly, when encountering a pungent smell or foul taste, e.g. your first oyster, the ego knows that it is not harmful and is OK to eat, the emotive sense responds by signally the body to repel the smell or taste and you may begin dry reaching.

The skin responds to the emotive sense of fear by the raising of the hairs on your body, or sensual arousal can make the skin tingle, eyes may glaze or voice become husky, even though the ego is denying that it has any desires of the person.

The unfortunate outcome for many people is when their ego is in control it will overcome those types of responses distributed throughout the body by the emotive sense by using anger or fear to overrule the thought.

I believe the emotive sense exists in all forms of animal especially humans. The difficulty for ego was that originally its only understanding for the emotive sense was what it experienced through the instinct. However, over the eons ego came to accept that the responses generated by the emotive sense were in fact a part of its make up that all information went direct through it to the brain for acting upon.

The other condition that exists in humans today is the substitute behaviours created by the ego as a replacement for the behaviours of the instinct.

Typical responses used everyday such as happy, sad, moody, bored, cheated, etc. that exist only within the ego at that moment for example, a fathers ego will be sad that his favourite team lost though his instinct filled with joy that he had spent the day sharing time with his son at the game.

As I see it there are seven areas of behaviour that the emotive sense responds in the life of humans and they are: "love" "anger" "fear" "intuition" "joy" "grief" and "character" with instinct and ego, having the capability to not only influence but also affect the balance of each.

These seven areas require the emotive sense to respond to the condition existing enabling the brain to activate the appropriate genes to create the chemicals and electrical impulses that will achieve the desired experience to every cell in the body and the following explanations will help make this clearer.

1. LOVE

Considered by many as the most important function of the human, love in one form or another affects every aspect of our existence with other humans, animals or plants we encounter in life from our conception until our death.

There are five basic different forms of love that the emotive sense is required to respond to: Parental, Self, Siblings, Friendships and Couples, and in each of the relationships it is possible for the "pure love" of Universal Energy existing within your body that was provided to you when creating your instinct to be present.

This love is within all of us to take advantage of to provide us with an existence we were born to have. The important aspect to understand is that this love is energy and as such, it is not something you can create and it is not possible to destroy it, only experience it.

It will not require an Albert Einstein to acknowledge the existence of each of these love relationships in the majority of animals as we look at each love type individually.

Be mindful that your ego struggles with this emotion because it is a part of the instinct, particularly if ego has been through the experience a failed relationship with any of the love forms.

For example, an exuberant ego wanting to have control can cause the breakup of the relationship, and then ego will turn to its opposite feeling of "hate" which it uses to shut down any feelings from a failed relationship.

PARENTAL LOVE

Instincts basic function with this form of love is for the protection of the young produced by a mating pair. Human behaviour for the relationship between the parent and child is for it to last a lifetime in the form of the family unit to ensure the colonisation of the species, which then acts as a protection mechanism of the species.

The emotive sense in both the parents and the child if in a loving relationship can respond to the feelings of "pure love" immediately upon conception being achieved.

It is also the first essential form of love experienced as a human being on the planet and as such, the loving experience received from parents or guardians is critical in forming a child's behaviour pattern.

Generally, the maternal emotive sense response is stronger than the paternal during the infant years of the child, more so on the part of the child than of the father most likely due to the child's instinct knowing the food chain supply. However, this balances out as the child's rational develops.

Ego controlled parents often display ownership, excessive pride issues or unrealistic expectations of their child in this relationship resulting in spoilt or repressed children which is not in the boundaries of pure love.

SELF LOVE

Instincts basic function of self-love is a "pure love" that the emotive sense responds to for the purpose of preservation of your very existence so that you do not place yourself in life threatening situations or cause harm to yourself unnecessarily.

It also ensures that you want your body to remain healthy, to live your full life cycle. With this essential form of love being our second to experience as a being, the role that the parents or guardians play in showing and teaching the child self love and self-respect is critical. the other role instinct plays for adults is in the search for a mate for the purpose of procreation, where it requires us to preen the body and perform the mating game to attract the one we are intending to set up house.

If instinct allows ego to influence too much control over this emotion, it has a tendency toward the extremes, resulting in the person being over vain and self absorbed at one end of the spectrum, to self-repulsion or self-abuse at the other end.

SIBLING LOVE

Instincts basic function in this form of love is in the teaching of bonding of the family unit for the protection of the family and the colony and includes family relatives in this group.

The love recognised by the response of the emotive sense in this relationship is also a "pure love" this is usually the third type of essential love experienced though not normally as strong as it is between couples or parent and child in most families depending on the reasons for the closeness formed in this relationship.

Many siblings are closest during their formative years particularly if the age difference is not too wide spread, and though it lasts a lifetime, often wanes to some degree when as adults pursue careers, marry and form their own family circle.

Ego is often very prevalent in this relationship in children, mainly due to the rivalry created trying to gain the approval of the parents and superiority or power over each other within the family group.

The adults in the family group need to control aggressive rivalry early, especially between young children before it can become a part of a child's character. It is also important that parents display equal levels of affection towards each of the siblings to reduce the ego condition of jealousy.

FRIENDSHIPS

Instincts basic function for this form of love is in the bonding of a colony through various degrees of what is termed "plutonic love" where the emotive sense response ensures romance or intimacy is not present between the close relationships of the couple regardless of their sex.

This relationship between the pair may last a lifetime or just a very short time, depending on the conditions that formed them and the lifestyle changes that end them which occur in many friendships.

For an only child this may be the third form of love experienced making it a priority for the parents to ensure they provide that opportunity.

In some instances, friendships can develop into a strong bond similar to that as it is between siblings as "pure love". In fact, some siblings also form this type of relationship between them for their entire life. Generally, it is a part of the independence needed to separate us from the other four forms of love, which is instincts way of teaching us to become individuals as well.

Allowing ego to dictate to much influence over this type of relationship can display the same tendencies of control and jealousy as that of couple's relationships.

The emotive sense responds the same where the relationship that exists between an owner and their pet animal form from this love category and in many instances will be equally as strong as that found between two humans.

COUPLES

Instincts basic function in the love formed between couples is for the purpose of procreation of the species, and the courtship rituals performed by the different races are often a fascination in itself. With the human being as with a number of species, the design of this relationship once formed is to last for the lifetime of the mating pair.

This relationship does not occur accidentally when you consider the number of people you meet during your life. How when that special someone comes along there is an immediate attraction that is different from a purely sexual response which ego can at times confuse as love, instead through the emotive sense, causes the body to react so differently than it does with any other person.

Your body's language tells you that this is that somebody special, regardless of how your ego is responding. Instinctively you know, and colour, age, creed, shape or size will not be a boundary. The use of the term "Soul mate" often describes the bond formed in this relationship. This bond is a result of the emotive sense playing a strong guiding role in maintaining the chemistry that only comes from "pure love". If ego dictates too much influence over this emotion, obsessive behavior is generally the outcome, resulting in various degrees of control or jealousy.

2. ANGER

Instincts basic function of anger is for the purpose of the protection of a species against the hazards and dangers faced in the fight for survival of one self, family and colony from the predators in their environment, territorial ownership by the species and their food sources.

The emotive sense signals all areas of the body when a threat is evident enabling the appropriate chemicals that increase strength, alertness and mobility to provide you with the best opportunity to ward off any such threat. Often in the case of protecting the family unit, will show extreme bravery and be willing to sacrifice one's owns life to protect the family unit, due to the fact that love is the stronger emotion.

The other function is to respond to any pain inflicted to the body, the instant you injure yourself however slight, the affected area notifies the emotive sense that then notifies every other cell in the body and the whole body responds in an act of defense.

Allowing ego to dominant over this emotion, rationality can be lost particularly when the issue is personal, and unrealistic reactions to everyday issues can arise, with some individuals aggressive behaviour reaching the point of uncontrolled rage in an effort to try to gain control over a situation.

3. FEAR

Instincts basic function of fear is also for the preservation of life of one's self, family and colony against the hazards & dangers of the environment and predators.

When the emotive sense receives a message from one or more of the other senses that indicates a life-threatening situation, the reaction is similar to the emotion of anger stimulating the body enabling you to respond to the threat however, to retreat rather than attack,

In its milder forms fear is to make you cautious, warning you of situations such as if, you are too high, the water is too deep, noise is too loud, etc. When the situation is extreme, this function can combine with anger, and then the chemicals and electrical impulses released enable the body to respond at speeds and strength rarely attainable.

This allows you to perform tasks beyond your normal abilities, and often there is no recall of the actions taken and achieved after the event by the ego, demonstrating that the ego plays little or no part at this level. There are examples of survival and heroism by ordinary people in disasters and war acted out daily on this planet.

When ego has control over this emotion, the outcome can result in cowardice or the total loss of rational thinking to the point of the individual "freezing up" i.e. complete confusion, unable to think clearly, to make a decision or in some instances even move their body.

4. INTUITION

Instincts basic function of intuition is to act as a forewarning system to the three previous types, especially in the areas of love or danger. The emotive sense responds when conditions and/or situations are present that one or all of our combined intelligence systems may have encountered, sending signals to all the body's cells to prepare to respond accordingly.

This system generally focuses on the areas of procreation, protection and preservation and is an essential part of the survival kit of all the animal species, including many plant species.

Common examples to observe, is that feeling when you meet someone for the first time and you just know that you would trust this person or the opposite situation where you feel unsafe that you cannot trust the person though you don't know their history.

I am always fascinated how ants build protection walls around their nest holes with the onset of coming rain, and always higher than the level of water on the ground from that rain.

We use intuition for many situations in our life commonly referred to as "gut feeling" or "heartfelt" often without us being aware influences our decisions on where we work, the town we live in, the house we buy, the friends we make, the list is quite long.

Unfortunately for many in today's society due to ego being allowed to be in total control, their intuitive skills are ignored, and premonitions of impending risks, even danger to themselves or their family, which was a basic skill of early humankind, are often overlooked much to their detriment.

Because of Egos non-acceptance of the existence of intuition it prefers to use words such as "luck" or "fate" to describe many of the intuitive results that arrive in our life that were not able to be logically explained by ego.

5. JOY

Instincts basic function for this condition is to provide an overall feeling of well being and contentment for the body or recovery after encountering any negative emotions. The emotive sense responds to the negative condition, activating the chemicals and electrical impulses, which stimulate the body's return to normal.

Some of the other main functions for joy are to enable the body to experience the natural contentment that is residing within the instinct in the gratitude at existing, or the general feeling of well being you experience when pure love is present. It also plays a role in the unity of the family and the colony especially in the area of communication skills where humour will often act as the bonding agent.

It is noteworthy that the intelligence system of ego and instinct respond differently when pleasurable conditions are present. Happiness defines egos response, which describes thoughts the ego experiences at that point in time.

Joy is a condition that the whole body experiences generated from the emotive sense response to love and/or character behaviour. For example, a mother will be joyous when handed her newborn child but may not be happy that it occurred in the taxi.

Ego often struggles to cope in this area especially when humourous comments cause doubt in its ability in areas of skill, intelligence or feelings, more so if ego is not in control of the humourous situation.

6. GRIEF

Instincts basic function for this condition is to provide a stress relief for the entire body, generally to overcome the distress experienced through the loss of a love in any of the love types, although in today's society the loss of material objects often receives the same level of distress.

When experiencing grief the emotive sense response activates the chemicals and electrical impulses, which are a mixture of love, anger and fear.

Instinct is required to perform two functions, firstly to regulate the counteracting chemicals to enable the body to gradually overcome those feelings of distress and continue with its life cycle.

While at the same time providing support for the ego, where in some cases the acceptance may take years to work through if at all, before it is able to cope with the loss.

Instinct needs to stay alert to ego thoughts of sadness, for it will continually express such thoughts to a personal loss gradually leading the body into a state of depression from the excessive amounts of chemicals that are continuously released.

In extreme cases in an ego-controlled person if the loss is the result of the death of a loved one in a devoted couple relationship, the trauma experienced by the surviving grieving body can be so devastating that the person affected by the grief can result in a heart attack.

7. CHARACTER

Instincts basic function for this is to be the controlling factor in the behaviour of any human. The ability of the emotive sense is such that it plays the major role in defining the behaviour needed which is associated with the situation in the body or acknowledged by one of the five physical senses.

For example, if your eyes observe another person to be ill, your emotive sense notifies the body including the instinct and ego to act in a caring, compassionate manner.

The main types of behaviours need listing so that it will help to understand the role of character you will need to act upon in part three of the book:

Caring, commitment, compassion, confidence, consideration, cooperation, courage, courtesy, determination, diligence, enthusiasm, flexibility, forgiveness, friendliness, gentleness, helpfulness, honesty, integrity, joyfulness, kindness, loyalty, moderation, orderliness, patience, peacefulness, perseverance, purposefulness, reliability, respect, responsibility, self discipline, service, tact, thankfulness, tolerance, trust, truthfulness, understanding, unity.

Quite an extensive list and you could probably add more if you wanted, the important point to observe is that one or more of these virtues are required for acting out or overcoming the areas of love, anger, fear, intuition, joy and grief that actually influence your behaviour patterns.

We perform many of these virtues listed above from the time we are a child, while some of the virtues may require almost the lifetime of an individual to be present some do not appear at all depending on the level of control the ego has.

Another aspect to observe is that the majority of these same virtues are also present in many species of the animal kingdom even where the ego plays only a minor role.

The reality is that you have all these virtues present in your instinct and you should be using these attributes whenever the condition arises. Except, instinct will not intentionally focus on any of those actions you perform only ego does, and constant acknowledgement by instinct appreciating any function of virtue performed by ego is to be encouraged.

The realisation is that just as the emotive sense is the main sense for a human being, character is the main guiding influence in that emotive sense. Your task is to convince ego of this when most likely at present, it prefers not to acknowledge the existence of either one.

THE GENES

One of the fascinating areas of instinct is the role it plays in the formation of our genes, upon conception, the miracle of life creates a marvelous being and although the mould is essentially the same for all humans, each is unique with their own identity.

For while the genes from the parents and their ancestors play a major role, instinct played a major role when creating gene cell formation, enabling enhancement of genes in some instances and deformation in others, providing the conditions for various types of health, talent and skill levels for each person.

These variations in each make it possible to be capable of functioning as the person they were born to be on this planet.

Science is now discovering the possibility that there is a gene for every function in our body; they are discovering also, that during the production of those cells, either there are those that will not be 100% perfect because of a fault during production of a gene or there can be a fault inherited from our ancestors.

This uniqueness, science identifies as our gene structure, is becoming more evident as one of the major areas for humankind to be researching to trace the health and the unique intricacies of the development and management of the body in all beings.

Eventually if medical science has the ability to eliminate all hereditary gene faults then humankind would only need to correct the ones that occurred during the production of the body, and by correcting those at an early stage, would create a society that nature probably had in mind in the beginning.

Many of the answers to understand the human body are in our genes and we can look at some examples of my nonprofessional thoughts that I believe may be influencing behaviour patterns.

HEALTH

The genes experts now find that many people with illnesses where a cause could not be identified result from inheriting faulty genes as the main cause of their disease, making it important to know the demise of your ancestors. While for others through a faulty or in some instances, possibly a missing gene allows the disease to develop rather than from any outside source.

One area to consider is the condition of obesity, if certain areas of the body are deficient in vitamins or minerals the genes request the brain to supply them but if the gene is faulty then possibly the request is non-stop providing a constant request to eat, particularly if it is for the fat cells.

Another area I believe is a major area of health for those gene experts to pursue is that of addiction, now recognised as an illness for anyone with an uncontrollable obsession be it substance, food, objects, sex, etc. When the gene that controls the addictive functionality can be isolated and corrected will stabilise many dysfunctional humans.

LOVE

Just as in health, the function for the five different forms of love requires genes to activate the appropriate chemicals and electrical impulses. I believe faults occur in these genes just as they do in health and in the same way i.e. hereditary or production faults.

For example, the possibility that genes meant for providing arousal between mating couples, instead activate one of the other types of love relationships. If true isolating and correcting these faults would provide opportunities to eliminate many of what society classify as dysfunctional sexual disorders existing today.

Another possibility to consider is if through a gene fault, an individual is unable to express or accept, one of the five types of love into their lives. Instead releases chemicals belonging to another of the emotional forms i.e. anger, fear, and grief which then takes us into the fields of physical, mental or emotional abuse, which I'm sure was not included in the design of any animal.

TALENT

From conception, our talent genes also aide in our physique and mental structure that will assist in using our talents through our life cycle, many talent genes are hereditary, many are common, but some genes are always special, special in a way that makes each individual unique. In some cases, they are extra special and this enables the various categories of champions, geniuses, leaders, etc.

Unfortunately, in this ego focused world of money or fear of failure, many of the people that despite having their special talents often do not get the opportunity to pursue them. For the majority of humans their unique talents are most likely suppressed becoming nothing more than a daydream or at best a hobby.

In general the education system is content producing en mass, people to perform routine tasks, who then, only if their desire is great enough and their will determine enough, are left to their own devices to pursue the talent with which they have been gifted. Imagine the life satisfaction possible if schools evaluated talents then directed the child's education and career towards those talents.

By the time, many children reach school age they often display special talents be it singing, acting, mathematics, sports to name a few. Would it not be better for that person to include in their schooling the talent they exhibit, rather than waiting until their school years are finished before given the opportunity to learn that field?

In today's world of the internet and television talent shows, it is quite apparent that many people have missed the opportunity to engage their unique skills because they had confined them to family fun days.

I believe that all schoolchildren need to undergo annual tests that would highlight the areas to direct where their talents best be suited and their school curriculum should reflect that.

Talents need to be steered in the right direction from a young age then the ego would readily accept this as the norm and would naturally steer itself in search of the direction of achieving the ultimate success, for being successful is the one category that will drive the ego forward with the minimal amount of resistance.

TELEPATHY

One of the genes humankind possesses but does not in general knowingly use today is the lost art of telepathy, excepting for some indigenous groups not affected by modern society, and most of the animal kingdom.

The reason modern man has lost this ability again unfortunately is ego's mistrust of any instinct capabilities that do not belong to the five physical senses responses. If you think about the person closest to you in your life how you discover that, you have both been having the same thought at the same time this is when telepathy is at work.

Another example is how a newborn child is able to draw its mother's attention to itself often without the aid of tears or sound; this mother/child mental communication observation is stronger in the animal kingdom especially when it comes to protecting the young or controlling their movements.

In addition, I have watched with fascination when observing two or more toddlers playing together and communicating while having no verbal skills, appearing to use only their eyes and hand gestures.

What I also consider a form of telepathy are clairvoyants, those people who claim to have the ability to seeing into our past, our future or to communicate with relatives and friends that are no longer living.

While there are many charlatans who like to prey on anyone willing to listen and part with their money, there are those who have proven they possess various levels of skill in this area.

If you agree it is possible to enhance some genes in preference to others as discussed earlier then it is reasonable to consider that if this gene is still active in most of us at varying degrees then some people would possess a high level of skill.

Therefore, if your enhanced telepathy gene were above average level, this would give you the ability to read some of the thoughts projected from a person who is in close proximity. That you could pick up personal information about a person's future desires, or information they were thinking about from their past.

Particularly, when you reminded them of a name, a deceased love one or perhaps information about the disappearance of someone who was close to them, provided they were a willing subject to divulge that information, which is what, is required for information to pass between two people through telepathy.

The very intriguing cases, which I have to say, are a difficult concept to comprehend, are those extremely special people who to me have the ability to be able to capture the intelligence energy of a person unknown to them who generally has died in a savage or unusual manner.

Somehow, they are able to receive the details of that person's intelligence energy and their last moments of life, and even lead police to their body. For it must be similar to releasing a droplet of water into the ocean and then recovering that very same droplet.

I have to restate that these people must be extremely special, unexplainable to some, but there have been cases proven, so I have to accept that this is possible, indicating that some form of intelligent energy exists after death which does no harm to my two theories that I have alluded to earlier.

However, I cannot accept that every human being that has died still "exists" on another plane with all his or her faculties intact as the person he or she once was. If this were the case, there must now be an uncountable number of spiritual beings in this plane, craving for the opportunity to communicate with anyone on this side capable of contacting them.

Moreover, if you consider that if those mediums who claim they physically see and speak to all these spirits supposedly still in human form, if it were possible to have such masses seeking your attention constantly, I doubt if any rational person would be able to withstand mentally.

Another area to consider is the possibility of our intuition and telepathic capabilities working in unison, creating the condition, where we attract people or conditions to bring changes into our life.

Especially if you have ever encountered the condition where, when you needed advice or help that, the right person appeared, or the exact condition arrived in your life to provide that very help or advice.

This to me now seems a more acceptable explanation rather than my concept in younger years of guardian angels floating around me, protecting me and assisting me in life's endeavor.

The revival and/or enhancement of the genes just discussed and the many others that science are now looking at, such as the age gene, cancer genes, fat gene, etc. without a doubt has to be the one of the main focuses forward for the future of a better humankind.

Once medical scientists are able to identify each of the genes we possess there will be many other areas to use in the field of help and support for better communication and understanding of each other. In addition, it may even be possible to establish some form of communication or at least better understanding of the rest of the animal kingdom.

Though I have barely touched on the possibilities of the gene field, it is plain to see that there are enormous opportunities to improve the quality of life far beyond the standards we have come to accept today.

CHAPTER 6

EGO CHARACTERISTICS

Today's human being depends on the ego intelligence more than ever before; it has become so much a part of our functionality that even though all our mobility is originally instinct driven it allows ego to control those functions unless life-threatening situations are present.

Instinct also allows ego to have control of our thought patterns unless those thoughts are placing the body in danger, even then in some instances is not able to overrule the ego thoughts.

Our instinct intelligence at the basic level is the same for all human beings, but of course varies in each individual due to dosage rate of anything for a body ever being the same.

It is the same with ego intelligence, resulting in the formation of various categories of ego behaviour, and each category generally have positive or negative outlooks on life.

The issue for you is to determine to what extent some outlooks that exist in your life or more precisely the behaviours, which are preventing you from achieving the fruitful life you were born to have.

There will of course be composites of the categories depending on the influence your ego currently has on your behaviour and you may see yourself in-between categories or likewise a mix of types even if only slight.

It is important to know which category you fit into in terms of any negative behaviours that are influencing your character. As part of your development, you need to review each of the categories of behaviour below and determine where you see that you best fit even if you need to compose your own mixed category.

You have to know the person you are at this point in order for you to be able to make any improvements that are not representative of your true self.

It is critical that you are very honest with your assessment; we all have behavioural faults or shortcomings in our character that have developed over time.

However, there is a very appropriate saying "you cannot change what you do not recognise" and you may need to revisit this section occasionally to reassess your assessment as to where you have changed.

The definitions in the following list in my view are the ones to consider as the main negative behaviours seen from day to day but do not be afraid to add any habit that I missed.

NEGATIVE EGO BEHAVIOUR

THE GUIDED

At first glance, this type appears to be content with everything that is happening in their life. Mostly because they believe that, the outcomes in life they achieve are the result of guidance from an outside source.

They receive their guidance through mediums such as religion, astrology, numerology, tarot cards, etc. that they believe is the major influence in their life and is serving their best interests. They generally do not trust them self to make lifestyle decisions, any decisions made by this type will seek approval first by their preferred source.

This lifestyle results in them being non-proactive resulting in missing many opportunities activating jealousy or envy behaviour patterns. A typical example is that job promotion that they could have applied for but did not, was not because someone else deserved the position more than they did, or was better qualified, but because their guiding source had not predicted this outcome for them and they have to have faith and patience for when their opportunity will arrive.

THE SOURPUSS

This type will tend to have negative opinions on many aspects in their life having little confidence in them self or their ability, because of this have difficulty making a decision. Most all their decisions follow by the question "But, what if?"

Some will always find a reason not to try anything new or different in their life not liking change preferring routine, for they are sure that if they do, something will go wrong preventing it from either eventuating or lasting. A favourite saying for them is "if it ain't broke don't fix it"

For some their negativity applies even to their own daily routines. A typical example is leaving home early for work at the same time each day, because they are certain if they change their time, the car will break down, be involved in an accident or that they might be caught in a traffic jam to make them late or, or, the negative reasoning seems to be endless.

This type can also have a tendency to be quite prejudice of everyone and everything, even to the point of racial and/or religious bias, but revealed only within the circle of accepted acquaintances.

THE COMPETITOR

This type will see everything that is happening in their life as a competition and the need to win is their prime objective, will often seem as impetuous with little regard of the effects that it can have on themselves or others. They will not have any problem in resorting to dubious tactics if the threat of losing becomes apparent, as they must be the best and have the best, often appears as being vain.

Typical examples can be from something as simple as to attempt cheating to ensure they achieve a winning result for themselves during a family board game or computer game, to being able to defame someone's character at work in order to gain that promotion or bosses approval for them self.

These types can suffer with "Keeping up with the Jones'" syndrome for some to the point of bankruptcy in their desire to have and be the best.

Generally see anyone outside his or her immediate circle, as inferior, whether it is the next-door neighbour, town, country, race or religion resulting in antisocial or racial behaviour toward anyone he or she feel threaten their self proclaimed superiority.

THE WORRYWART

For this type, every aspect of life is a drama, concerned about anything and everything, finding it difficult to finalise or accept any decision or direction in their daily life because of perceived fears of the possible outcomes for themselves or the world.

It is extremely difficult for them not to worry, even brooding the whole day over simple tasks such as having turned off an appliance or locked the garage door when they left the house, to the constant concern with the threat of nuclear annihilation.

This type of behaviour in the extreme becomes an illness rendering the person incapable of living a normal life too afraid to accept or provide a rational thought on anything happening in their life.

THE PLANNER

There is no way that this type of person could even get out of bed each day unless they had set out a plan at least the day before. For these people organisation is everything and they will often have perfectionist tendencies, and once they lay out their program then any disruption to that plan is devastating.

These people enjoy organising everything and everybody, being poor listeners as they are planning their next sentence while someone else is speaking. Find it offensive when anyone rejects his or her plan, they know their plan is the right one for their time is too valuable for poor planning.

They always need to carry an electronic planner or at least a diary to refer to before committing themselves to any new activity, because their time is set out for months' in advance.

THE AGGRESSOR

This type seem to prefer to live with their blood pressure level at its upper limits and are becoming more prevalent in today's society. They not only appear to be, but actually are angry with everyone and everything including themselves.

Highly stressed due to their impatience they are the ones involved in the various forms of anger we see more of in today's society typically such categories as road rage, trolley rage, etc.

These people are typically quite stubborn viewing themselves as always being right and they view anyone who disagrees with them as the enemy.

In fact, being self-righteous they see anything that does not place them in a positive light as personal attacks on their character or their ability and will strike out verbally or physically, before any explanations or reasoning are given.

The most dangerous when in the extreme but even in its mild form this behaviour can make life difficult for anyone not complying with his or her beliefs, typically in such things as race, religion, cultures or customs or at a minimum uncomfortable being around them.

THE FEARFUL

This type tend to live in fear of everyone and everything especially where responsibility or decision-making is required diverting their path as far as need be required in order to avoid any form of confrontation.

They often find it difficult to say no to anyone even though they know that they are unable to fulfill the commitment, just so others will not question them.

For some people it is all about anonymity, they are prepared to participate as long as they remain unnoticed. If they are singled out to make a comment, decision or respond to any situation, will become embarrassed, flustered or freeze up.

They are usually happy to be the workhorses in any group, which makes them the focus of the leader type so that he or she attains their goal.

They are usually quite adverse to pain and seem to suffer more illnesses than others do, can sometimes tend to have hypochondriac tendencies.

THE ARROGANT

This type are the result of poor parenting that is becoming all too regular in today's society due to the parents wanting to befriend their children allowing them everything they desire with little training if any in discipline or manners.

These children grow up with an exaggerated sense of their own importance and ability, generally, very self-opinionated with little tolerance for other people's needs or welfare.

This type are usually selfish resulting in an expectation that their needs require attention first, and will become aggressive and sarcastic if they are not which shows them as being rude and insolent.

THE BLASÉ

This type does not concern themselves with the issues of daily life routines, money issues, people's opinions or the like. Instead, content to go about their life oblivious to the needs of others with little regard for the effects they incur on the rest of the community.

This type of person can also have poor personal hygiene habits or poor work ethics requiring someone else to be responsible for them.

Have an expectation that it is the responsibility of the government to care for them.

THE FAILURE

For this type, there is no point in attempting to try to achieve anything, because they know that anything they attempt is only going to fail, that everyone and everything is against them including god, fate, karma or any other source. Each time there seemed that an opportunity came up and it was going to improve life; some new disaster came along and put them back in the mire.

This type will often turn to food or substance abuse to compensate for their low self-esteem and usually have little difficulty placing the blame on others for their position in life.

THE PROCRASTINATOR

For this type time is their worst enemy; time restricts them from spending their days doing what they prefer to be doing, when they feel like they want to do it. These people tend to be dreamers, are generally quite disorganised, rarely on time for an appointment, preferring to make decisions about their day at the last moment, often will spend their whole weekend deciding how they intend to spend their time, without ever leaving the lounge chair.

THE LEADER

This type stands out in the crowd, they are the decision makers, their opinion is the only right one, every task requires their approval, and in their eyes for most situations, they will have a better idea than anyone else will.

They will always be prepared to argue their case as being the best option to pursue even to the point of refusing to be involved in an activity unless their idea forms part of the final decision accepted; for a group activity, they also have to appear to be in control if it is to achieve any success. They were often a bully while growing up and are still inclined to prefer that method of control.

THOUGHTS FOR CHANGE

The first step to improvement in any area of your life is to recognise that a fault currently exists, and although you may not be able to change that behaviour at this point, it might be possible to start making some readjustments that will enable a more balanced ego. Below is a range of thoughts that can help provide direction for that balance.

THE GUIDED

Endeavouring to have a positive outlook for your self is a good thing in all aspects involved with living a life of contentment. However, it is critical that you "know" that you are the only one that can produce any outcomes to provide that life, that any dependence on outside sources is futile. Make a decision on an easy project without seeking your medium's advice, and then take the next step and act without asking your medium. Then do another project. Learn, understand and employ the word "confidence"

THE SOURPUSS

Of course viewing every aspect of your life in a negative frame certainly provides no opportunity for you to produce positive outcomes. Routine may be comfortable but change is happening around you and with you at every moment if you were to pay more attention to your surroundings.

The first step is to have less concern for the behaviours of others, you can only be responsible for what you say and do. The question you need to ask yourself is if the behaviours of others that offend you, are actually the faults you see in you.

THE COMPETITOR

Being competitive is a healthy condition to employ in business and sporting situations, as it increases the chance to achieve positive results. It is easier to cheat if you have no self-respect, by remaining true to yourself and accepting any outcomes whether in your favour or not makes winning or losing enjoyable for everyone if done fairly.

Unless you are in the billionaires club and have attained the level of religious master trying to best everyone is pure futility, learning to live in contentment with your self is your prime objective. Learn, understand and employ the word "respect"

THE FAILURE

It is easier to give up when you do not get what you want, in addition, blaming others for your failures may provide some comfort. Attempting any project with a negative approach will surely produce a negative result, but if you never try, then you will never know and self-abuse of your body will bring more pain than failing in the long term. Instead, learn from the mistakes, you need to keep trying until you experience the joy of obtaining a successful result. Learn, understand and employ the word "diligence"

THE PLANNER

Everybody has plans, some achievable some not. It is essential however, that plans are flexible enough that they do not impede on you having a contented life or impose on the life of others. Start small; try planning days where you have no plan for that day, do nothing, and keep on doing it until it feels good doing nothing if only for a short time. Learn, understand and employ the word "moderation"

THE PROCRASTINATOR

To daydream your life away affects no one but you, but ensure any lack of concern for plans or time spent by you not imposes on the plans and activities of others in your life, as both behaviours can cost you good friendships, family even jobs. The first step to change is to learn, understand and employ the word "consideration."

THE AGGRESSOR

Many people in society today need to take a deep breath and just listen to the ranting thoughts of their impatient ego before they open their mouth. I know that many say they are embarrassed after the fact, feeling silly with some of the words spoken.

It is not possible that you are always the most important person on the planet that everyone has to move aside for you. The harm you are doing to your body when in constant stress takes years off your life expectancy, start practicing the use of deep breathing techniques to calm your thoughts. Learn, understand and employ the word "patience"

THE FEARFUL

Stress is just as harmful to the body for those living in constant fear to face their own life or other people in their life. If you start saying no to the things you cannot achieve it will be easier to say no to the things you do not want to achieve. Consider joining a gym or self-defense class to obtain a more positive outlook even just to improve your health.

THE ARROGANT

Change for this ego type will not be an easy road, as your ego has known no difference; the first steps that will most likely assist you is to engage in practicing one of the moderate martial art forms that focus on "tolerance and caring" behaviour.

THE LEADER

Every group needs a leader especially in the work place. However, it is important that the group for the best results make the decisions. Moreover, that everyone is involved in the final decision, particularly if it is a social function for family or friends. Your first step is "learning to listen" many people out there have some great ideas and opinions equally important to them.

THE FOLLOWER

Every group needs workhorses and it can be satisfying to be involved in a project, but if you are not enjoying it, especially if you had a better approach to make the project successful if you had only said something. Then it may pay you to make your next project a speech course or some similar course else all your good ideas will never be heard.

THE BLASÉ

While appearing to be a good life if you did not have a care in the world, the reality is the opposite, by expanding your "caring" behaviour pattern appreciating all that is in your life will provide you with more contentment in your life and for those who currently have to cover for you.

THE WORRYWART

On the opposite hand worrying does not get it done, when a situation arises that is concerning you, be proactive and do something about it before those stress levels harm you. It may be to your advantage to learn a meditation practice to enable those worrying thoughts to dissipate through a method controlled by you.

EGO MISCONCEPTIONS

As you have been reading the previous chapters I am certain that you have been discussing this concept of a being in the being with yourself. The question often asked is, who is talking to whom. Me, I have no doubts, I am sure in my heart of hearts as the saying goes.

Have you ever noticed when it comes to making an important decision people will say "Do what your heart tells you", "go with your gut feeling" ego tries to disassociate itself from those difficult decisions, leaving them to instinct, that way if the decision doesn't work ego will not be the blame. From these conclusions, I believe some other important misconceptions by the ego have an effect on the behaviour of humans today and we can review these now.

Because instinct is prepared to base the majority of its thoughts on survival allows ego to focus on its own interpretation of the senses. From the early development of the ego area of the brains expanding knowledge, when the whole body responded "instinctively" to any information received from any of the senses, the ego accepted that information was fact that these senses were trustworthy.

The ego acknowledges its dependence on the five physical senses as crucial to its survival. However, it is very different with the ego when it comes to understanding the emotive sense.

The misconception that the reaction from one of the physical senses, went first to its area of the brain for a decision then to the rest of the body, rather than via the emotive sense direct to every cell in the body, is the first major distorted view the ego has to overcome.

I believe immediate response is required from all the organs needed at once, e.g. heart, lungs, chemical release, muscle movement, skin, etc. that all have to function at the same time as the brain when a response is required for any movement of the body.

The second major misconception is ego's belief that through the brain it controls the functions of all the organs of the body. I believe there is evidence that shows this is not true especially when someone has received serious 'brain damage' resulting in deep coma.

This damage results in total loss of the ego intelligence; reducing the person to the condition given in nonprofessional terms as "being a vegetable" in other words, the body is relying on the instinct intelligence existing within the brain as the connection to the body's organs to continue functioning.

The third major misconception is the failure of ego to accept the role that instinct plays in our life, assuming all thoughts and actions result from the ego learning's, and it is true that many of the creative lessons learned by ego throughout human evolution have been instilled into our instinct to advance our species.

However, as I stated earlier "nature" upon conception, provides those learned skills, originally provided for as part of the instincts ability that must be learned by ego.

This in my opinion explains best my theory of our instinct energy role after our death that the information, which provided our instincts, returns to nature who then installs it into the next generation of instinct intelligence in humans. Especially when you observe how newborns are readily able to accept the surroundings and technology of today's world.

Despite this failure to accept instinct by the collective ego in general, in some circles parent's for centuries have been attempting to match up specific natural skills or intelligence aspects such as education, music, science, sport, etc. when searching for the perfect mate for their children. In the hope or expectation that the offspring will perform, the enhanced skill that the perfect mate possesses.

The fourth major misconception is ego's belief that it does not die when the life cycle of its body is complete that it remains an individual becoming a part of a universal spiritual system.

The reality for me is that only instincts intelligence energy remains after death but is required to return to its origin to ensure all remains in balance. For ego, its creation evolved over eons of time for each species of animal within the brain, and when the brain dies so does the ego.

Many mistakenly refer to the term defining the universal intelligence energy component in our body, as the "spirit" which ego claimed so it could maintain its sense of superiority.

When in fact, as stated earlier this intelligence energy is beyond the realms of humankind especially the physical senses of communication, instead one of knowing that "pure love" exists here, that it is everywhere and it is in control of all that exists.

Despite many investigations by the most reliable sources available on the existence of the afterlife, no one has produced any significant evidence to prove or reject the concept totally.

I suggested earlier with my theory that because we do know that we cannot destroy energy that the feasibility of our energies existing after death is a reality the question is in what form.

The possibility of one or all of our energies that formed our instinct remaining intact after death and capable of contact, then communicated with, is a difficult concept to accept.

We still need to understand the "miracle of life" and once that happens the existence of or in what form our energy exists after death may become clearer.

I believe telepathy will play a major role through the talents of those with that gene enhanced who possibly could access the sub conscience of willing subjects to reveal details of our evolution.

The fifth major misconception of the ego is due to its desire for counteracting the behaviour patterns of the instinct, which has resulted in the highest distortion of the ego intelligence and our relationships with each other.

As stated earlier, the ego examines and re-examines the information stored in its sub conscience plus the teachings and the behaviours of others, then claims ownership of all it learned.

The unfortunate result is that ego obtains all the behaviours both good and bad then analyses all that knowledge, to the extreme ends of positive and negative possibilities, it is then practiced to the level the ego experiences or the definition determined by the ego.

Some I have already raised where the ego for its own purpose creates its own combinations of feelings from the seven areas of the instinct i.e. Love, anger, Fear, Intuition, Joy, grief and character. While we could create a dictionary on the various combinations commonly formed, we should at least review a few of the more serious negative ones from ego to get the picture.

HATE—The combination of conditions experienced through grief from a lost love, the fear of losing, the anger at failure or inability to control such characteristics as tolerance, loyalty, understanding, etc.

GREED—Thoughts of lack or fear of losing what the person has gained, resulting in negative thoughts of the characteristics of self-discipline, trust, compassion, integrity, etc.

LUST—Over focusing on the sexual pleasures derived from Love by a couple during copulation, resulting in the negative thoughts in characteristics of self-discipline, respect, caring, understanding, responsibility, etc.

ENVY—thoughts of lack combined with anger from the inability in controlling patience, perseverance, cooperation, commitment characteristics.

WORRY—When the fear of not being in control of situations and the characteristic of diligence, flexibility, orderliness.

JEALOUSY—The condition experienced when hate combines with conditions such as greed, lust or envy.

BULLYING—The condition where low self-love combines with hate, jealousy and deriving pleasure from creating fear and anguish in other people.

As you may have observed, this will be quite an extensive list if you consider that, for every experience recorded by humans and a judgment made resulted in the possibility of an extreme thought by the ego, with many of the final decisions being negative rather than positive.

Moreover, in many cases not really a part of the actual situations or conditions, especially when those thoughts related to personal matters.

The other aspect to observe is that the negative behaviour starts to emerge when a child reaches the age of two years thus the phenomenon of the terrible two's, that if left to run its own course creates a child difficult to control right through to adulthood.

EGO ANOMALIES

There are many scenarios and conditions in our life that are accepted into the range of "normal" situations that we are all aware of, but are subjects the ego has no valid answers for, instead prefers us to accept and not question or think about at all.

Mostly they are questions that are either in the too "hard basket" or in some instances labeled as taboo subjects by ego as there is no explanation it can provide. When these types of queries face us, the ego will generally respond with anger or fear to close down the subject.

However, I believe that these subjects' best explain the existence of our instinct which an ego controlled mind fights hard to disagree with, especially when it sees instinct having any degree of recognition. Many of these types of thoughts influence the way human behaviour mannerisms have developed, so let's review a few.

LANGUAGE

An infant child's ego intelligence has to learn the language of its guardians but it quite clearly has thoughts and makes decisions long before it is able to communicate by speech. In other words, our instinct has a language when we are born.

We consider the art of communication a feature of human beings, mainly because we do not have the ability to learn the language of any other animal. However, if you have owned a pet or observed animals you would agree that animals think and make decisions, and to do so they need a language. In other words, their instinct has a language.

Therefore, in my mind, the language of instinct has to exist; the unknown factor is if it is a common language, which is possible as it comes from the same source for each species. Another possibility is because the instinct provided in the DNA of a species is peculiar to the species, and then the language is as well, which enhances my theory on instinct intelligence returning to nature.

Until recent times humankind had denied this feature of instinct particularly in animals even to the point of claiming all other animals to be dumb and not capable of intelligent thoughts, which then allowed ego controlled humans the right to treat other animals in whatever manner they desired.

DREAMS

In earlier chapters, I proposed how aspects of our body and instinct intelligence are the result of our ancestors, and that much of humankind's history still exists in our sub conscience.

With this in mind and knowing, our sub conscience never sleeps, being instincts part of the brain that needs to cooperate with all our other organs.

In addition, knowing that our ego part of the brain requires sleep daily to function correctly, requires acceptance that instinct is in control while ego sleeps reviewing knowledge gained by ego since it last slept deciding if or where that information needs recording.

That accepted information then copied into the sub conscience for storing, then I believe many of the dreams we have come directly from our sub conscience that is replaying information for updating that formed part of the information you received at conception.

This opens up the possibility that may explain those unusual dreams we have where we have found ourselves in places that we are certain we have never been. Equally, involved with people that we have never met, languages we do not speak and engaged in activities we have never done.

My reasoning for why we do not usually remember dreams is because ego requires less sleep than the rest of the body and once ego awakens it will regain control and influence any thoughts currently flowing from your instinct, so that when we awake almost instantly we cannot remember.

In addition, if ego is woken and struggling to regain control induces negative thoughts into the dream such as falling or drowning resulting in what we term a "nightmare" or "night terror" in order to wake the rest of the body particularly the senses, which without it feels threatened.

One area I would like you to consider that your ego will not accept is the situation if you have experienced when you had a dream about an event or situation before it actually happened.

To me this indicates your intuition was functioning while you slept and provided you with information of the upcoming event that you were able to respond to rationally because you knew what was happening next.

DEATH

Each of us is born with an age gene and those fortunate enough to survive their full life cycle appear to accept death in a peaceful manner, as do those who accept their impending death due to a terminal illness or injury that will reduce their natural life cycle.

Without a doubt, our egos' biggest fear is death because it cannot accept that it will no longer exist once death occurs. This failure to accept death as final has resulted in humankind creating various forms of afterlife havens throughout many religious cultures,

Each of these cultures perform a ritual to ensure that the "soul" of believers reach that afterlife haven with all their faculties intact. Of course, the paths for non-believers as far as believers are concerned, still have their faculties intact but their path is one of an eternity of despair, fear and loneliness or for the wicked, an eternity of torture, dread and mayhem to endure.

I believe our death cycle actually follows the same path as our creation cycle, by that I mean just as at our conception into our DNA the instinctive intelligence was added then at our death the last thing to leave us is our instinctive intelligence.

Accepting that ego only commences functioning after our birth to eliminate ego's fear behaviour makes it easier to realise why ego thoughts are also the first to cease functioning in the death cycle.

This to me explains how the people who have survived a near death experience, saying they saw their life flash before their eyes, followed by a bright light then a peace unknown before.

This experience best answered as their instinct in the process of closing down the body through the point in time when it first witnessed the presence of light until only the intelligence energy existing in their major organs remained. The only reason these people survived death was that instinct was still functioning in their organs, enabling their revival.

This shutting down period of the body is sequential and once oxygen ceases flowing to the brain, the ego area only has minutes for revival before starting to deteriorate and ego skills are lost whereas instinct has to depart the body.

The ability for determining when the instinct actually departs the body is an area where medical science focuses their attention, for it provides valuable information to the doctors and ambulance staff at what point resuscitation attempts are no longer a viable option or on a patient volunteering their body for transplant purposes.

When the instinct completely leaves the body that life has ended, and the only way any physical part of the body can survive an impending death is by transplanting it into another living body before this occurs.

Today transplants provide the ability for thousands of people to live normal lives, and the day will come when society accepts as routine when doctors will perform transplants without having to obtain approval from anyone other than the provider for those parts.

Included in this category of routine will also be the need for acceptance of stem cell replacement, but it will require the cumulative ego of society to accept before either can become a reality.

SPIRITS AND GHOSTS

This is probably the best time to discuss the spirit world while death is fresh in our mind. The ego fears the unknown so to compensate the ego theorises explanations for every condition, and of course, death is at the top of the list.

The collective ego of humankind concluded that there had to be an afterlife for them to remain in existence and that there needed to be a haven much better than life on earth for those who were deserving of it, and equally a place to extricate those to another place who were not.

This required the creation of a physical form thus the spirit (for the good) and the ghost (for the bad) those poor souls who have failed to meet the criteria of a good spirit and their penance is to haunt the living to ensure the living will follow the path of goodness.

The creations of these philosophies were in a time when people were more gullible to their fears of death and accepted these ideas as truth because they came from people that ruled over them. As most could neither read nor write the words of kings, and high priests were law, besides, disagreeing openly or daring to question their rules you were most likely put to death.

When you consider ego's fear of the dark, because it reduces one of its most trusted features "sight" add in the "sounds" of expanding or contracting buildings, nocturnal animals or shapes formed by fog, mist, wind, etc. they all added up to those feared creatures "ghosts".

These philosophies at the time were a good thing because it enabled societies to be able to exist where people believed that if they were good in life then life would be good in death and it was easy to create ghosts to prove it. In addition, this helped redirect the behavioural nature of humankind of those times.

Nonetheless, it is not OK for practicing these spirit and ghost concoctions today, especially for the purpose of fear tactics to control children's behaviour at night, as these fears are ego based that can have an effect on their behaviour mannerisms when adults.

Uncountable numbers of people claim to have witnessed the existence of spirits good and evil, which makes them difficult to discount. In addition, if a clairvoyant can contact the intelligence energy of a lost life then discounting them entirely would be a mistake.

To me this phenomenon falls into the same category as aliens in that, for some reason you have to believe in it before you are able to experience it and non-believers can please themselves.

REINCARNATION

It follows that if there is a spirit world then ego can make the next extreme thought and be reborn again, especially if achieving recognition in a previous life that entitles them to return and continue their work.

Some people place themselves under hypnosis and while in this state are able to speak fluently in a language previously unknown or recall experiencing events that occurred before their current life with such accuracy suggesting this provides the proof of their earlier existence.

For me this condition helps support my suggested theory that all of the instinctive knowledge of our predecessor's passes over to nature on their death, then at our conception provided to us as instinctive intelligence. If someone does possess the talent to recall beyond this life, they are actually recalling information captured by nature from those predecessors and is present as part of their instinct rather than that they are an actual ancestor reborn.

This obviously is a very special talent and this particular skill is another that science should be seeking out, as this is the path to discover the true evolution of humankind, that there is certainly a real opportunity for us to explore more of our history through these people.

RELIGION

As far back as humankind can record, in every culture there has been religion in some form, even the most primitive of cultures accepted there was some form of Supreme Being responsible for their existence and worshiped this Supreme Being.

Unfortunately, due to humankind's ego the only true religion was the one that was victorious over another, generally through wars between the different tribes, races and countries in the process destroying the culture and beliefs of those defeated.

Therefore, down through the ages to enable the justification in the acceptance that the religion of one group was the true religion over another, people killed, maimed and tortured.

I would like to be able to say that thankfully today this is no longer the case, but I cannot, in truth we are not much further advanced than those of yester years in fact we are probably much worse off, because it is now set on a world platform that is effecting many thousands of innocent lives.

God and nature may have created humankind, but humankind created religion, and though we based the concept of religion on all the aspects of our instinct, the rightness and extremeness of the ego has defined all sorts of rules and boundaries which most people have difficulty living up to.

Another intriguing area for consideration is that many of the surviving religions of today have been in place for thousands of years, and most of the rules and boundaries had been set to create fear and compliance by intimidation to anyone who failed to conform to those ideals throughout those years.

If you accept that words like education, science, medicine, equality, freedom, etc. were at their very crudest and basic if at all when creating the religious philosophies. That in today's society the majority of those rules should be/are rejected more and more as an act of discrimination.

Logically you would consider that in today's society of educated levels unimaginable when the religious laws were set, that we could apply common sense to meet the needs of humankind today, especially when knowing the cruel methods that played a part in setting those old standards.

Even when considering the subject of the "afterlife" to this day there are still religious factions promising that those who obey the faith without question will receive an eternity of wonderment as their reward?

However, those that do not will still be outcast regardless of any good they achieve during their life, and this is where the ego is in its realm, because we are in the extreme and keeping alive the thoughts that will convince us our ego will live on beyond our death.

Maybe the sad part is that as humans we have not advanced enough in our behavior patterns since those times except that we are much more subtle generally in camouflaging the non-acceptance of the beliefs and cultures of others.

OUTER SPACE

An interesting point to consider regarding the concept of aliens and UFOs is that people have been making claims to them visiting this planet for any number of years, appearing on planet earth for short visits and heading off again.

In the last 100 years, believers have continually relocated the distance these aliens have travelled, in the early days of sightings they were inhabitants travelling back and forth from the moon. Then with education, the believers claimed that Mars must be their habitat, and now they believe the aliens must travel to and from other star systems or galaxies on a regular basis possibly through time tunnels.

Not once have they officially or openly tried to communicate to establish a dialogue, instead the only communication has been with those unfortunate souls they capture, torture and set loose again.

In truth, I cannot imagine how any civilization that were that technologically advanced to achieve such a task, would have any reason to fear any communication with us or that anything any human on this planet currently has that could threaten them.

I believe it is extremely unlikely that humans will ever have the necessary mental capacity to produce machines that could physically transport humankind, travelling through outer space at speeds proportional to the speed of light. Enabling us even reaching similar planets that exist in other star systems in this universe let alone to return to earth with the knowledge necessary to sustain life on this planet that will need providing to meet the over populated demands of the future.

While there is no doubt that, there are probably untold numbers of planets that meet that criterion; the distance to them is astronomical in terms of humankind's capabilities. This theory I am sure will not appease many of those who believe in the theory that we were all aliens, or those that believe we receive regular visits by aliens.

The real truth I believe is that space exploration is being pursued for the same reason many of our forefathers explored our planet, the search for riches and fame which are two categories adored by ego.

The possibility of returning from another planet in our solar system with precious stones or new metals is far more feasible than to return with a new species of food from another star system that would be capable of feeding the multitudes, particularly with the spacecraft of today.

This of course is a cynical view; however, when you consider the cost of the space program I once read that it was possible to irrigate large areas of Western Australia for farming, by installing channels to redirect the massive amount of water from their northern rivers received during the wet season that currently flows out to sea. If done could supply crops and grain to thousands of people.

Unfortunately, the authorities rejected the idea because it required several billion dollars to achieve and of course, no one had those kinds of funds available for a pie in the sky idea like that. It then begs the question of how many other countries have the ability to irrigate their land provided they had the funds to achieve it.

There are more examples of ego anomalies we could look at but these were the ones I thought play a big part in today's culture and also are the ones that we may be able to influence in our need to change humankind's behaviour on life.

PART 3

THE PERSON YOU WERE BORN TO BE

For people whose ego has dominated the thoughts in their life this section will be difficult in the beginning, unfortunately there is no easy path; the good news is that now you know there is more to your thoughts than you were aware.

In all probability, you may have struggled to contain egos negative responses right through part one and two. This will be far more intense for your ego because now it actually is required to provide instinct equal participation within your thought process on decisions.

If you have been taking notes, you now have a reasonable picture of the person you currently are and I am not suggesting that there is anything wrong with that person. For the majority of people, their ego character is who they are, directing many of their mannerisms and behavioral characteristics on a day-to-day basis.

For a number of people changing that person into the one you were born to be only requires subtle change, for as I said at the beginning of this book the majority of people act accordingly to their "conscience" thus instinct thoughts, you only need to do it more often and that now is your next goal.

For others up until the present point in time both systems will have been on separate paths, where instinct is content to focus on the groundwork of guiding the body through its life cycle, ensuring the continuation of the specie. Whereas ego's focus is mainly on achieving the most gratifying life possible for itself while on this earth.

In this existence, instinct will only attempt to redirect ego's thoughts from harm's way whenever ego's behaviour places the body in jeopardy such as overeating, substance abuse, stress, damage, etc.

In many cases when the emotive sense sends messages to warn of harmful conditions ego will often ignore these warnings, continuing on its own path of self-satisfaction, often regardless of whether that path is positive or negative, unless there is immediate life threatening conditions then instinct will act before ego begins to think.

In order to achieve the life of being the person you were born to be, it requires your intelligence systems to work in unison, that is, working towards a common goal that your instinct and ego will feel is a complete life.

The goal therefore is to train both to work together as a team for the benefit of your body, lifestyle, and eventually for your peace of mind.

This is not an overnight program but one that is achievable, one that should have a timetable placed on it, for you will need to complete this program in two stages and then requires constant review for the whole life cycle.

In the first stage, instinct's profile needs to be raised so that ego is more accepting of this other intelligence residing in your body, while at the same time convincing ego of the extra knowledge and skills usable, which instinct can provide that will improve your life.

This will require you to follow a method I call the three L's that seems to have gotten lost for many people in this fast moving world and that is to "look, listen, and learn" firstly within yourself, then to all other beings you encounter throughout your life.

Until you reach the level where ego and instinct can review their thoughts together calmly, then, and only then should you bring up the subject of the emotive sense, which is the real purpose of stage one. Training the ego to recognise and then accept this major component in your instinct will take practice and commitment, and like developing any skill, constant access is the key.

In the second stage, you will use those skills and knowledge gained with the guidance of instinct, that will enable you to pursue a life that ensures, when you are taking your last breaths in life, the ego will be just as content as instinct, with all of the memories and achievements completed in its life cycle.

An ego saying that will be needed to overcome is "believe nothing you hear and only half what you see" for while it may have some validation in our dealings with certain people in our lives, it certainly has no place in matters relating to the self.

In fact, it will be the opposite as one of the methods I discuss to resolve issues that arise in your progress in stage two is "stop" "look" and "listen" to review and overcome the doubts that certainly will appear in that part of your journey.

You will first need to identify the issues that currently exist between your instinct and ego that is currently restricting their interaction before you can raise the profile of your instinct. The degree to the length of time this will take is dependent on the number of issues you identify and resolve that currently exist between the two.

ISSUES FOR INSTINCT

While you have identified changes that your ego may need to correct up until this point, there also maybe major changes required of your instinct in order to enable their implementation.

The following issues are the ones that I see as the most likely to have affected your behaviour mannerisms to date when instinct has failed to take an active role.

The first major issue for your instinct to correct is in communication with the ego, for it will allow ego to control your thoughts even when it is clear that there is potential danger in the activity you are executing.

People will often say, "Something told me this would cause me grief" "but I ignored it" when explaining the after effects of an accident or incident.

The knowledge and skills in your instinct is far greater than that of ego and you have to do at least one of two things: either make your instinct more assertive or to teach ego to be a better listener. Truthfully, you will achieve a far more positive outcome if you can implement both.

The second issue for your instinct to overcome is complacency with ego, for instinct will allow ego to behave in a manner that it knows is outside the standards with which it is comfortable.

People will say "every bone in my body kept saying that what I was doing was wrong" "but I could not stop myself". However, because ego struggles with limitations and finds it easy to ignore those thoughts, your instinct is the only one who can reason with ego to keep your behavior standards in control, and it must learn to speak out. Particularly, in the condition of egos understanding of "fun" as there is a vast difference in the definition between the two schools of thoughts for some people.

The third issue is for your instinct to change its acceptance of ego mannerisms, anytime the ego is planning, scheming or making judgments about anything or anyone it is the role of instinct to keep the ego in check.

When people say "I didn't realise that what I said/did would cause any harm" then instinct is in fact complying with that action, by not raising the issues involved with ego to confront those proposed thoughts/actions only provides ego with the thought of approval.

The fourth issue for your instinct is to improve its perseverance with ego, when it becomes apparent that a project created by ego is also one that instinct is enjoying. It has to stand firm to overcome the complaining and lack of commitment by ego wanting to quit when immediate results are not forth coming. The saying "if at first you don't succeed, try, try, again" is not one created by or followed by ego, especially if any failures are involved.

The fifth issue for your instinct is being diligent with ego, for it is quite easy for instinct to be content to focus on what is happening right now. Therefore, if the body is performing to its requirements and its environment is safe, as far as instinct is concerned it is meeting its role. But the reality is that instinct also has to maintain its presence in every thought that ego is having, to ensure it is not only participating in the decision making but having an influence on those thoughts that control your behaviour.

One or all five of these issues may be present in your life today, and it will require you to participate in the activities throughout stage one to overcome a reluctant instinct that has most likely given up trying to indulge a controlling ego.

ISSUES FOR EGO

The continual rivalry by ego to control instinct has resulted in issues for all seven areas of the instinct that affect the behaviour of many humans and I will review these now. The challenge will be to allow instinct to participate in overcoming these issues through one of the virtues associated with its character, learning ego those virtues will provide the answers to these issues.

LOVE

There are several issues to overcome in this area and some of these issues have developed from a very young age while others are the results involving self-control.

Prior to World War 1, the female ego had for the most part remained repressed by many races and religious societies, whereas most expected free expression of the male ego. However, since then that has changed in many societies and today's woman expect that they have the same behavioral rights as men, although some races and religions still scorn such rights.

A significant effect has flowed from this change and this new freedom has enabled women to perform tasks and live lifestyles once regarded as for men only. Unfortunately, in many situations both men and women are struggling to deal with this equality, often resulting in the breakdown of the family unit when the overzealous egos of each attempt to take control.

Communication is the key to understanding the needs and feelings of each followed by flexibility in the give and take that is required in any relationship.

One of the main problems stemming from the development of a more permissive and equal society is with couples focusing on the pleasures achieved in their sexual activities and confusing this as a true loving relationship. However, once the pleasures begin to wane, ego controlled types then start the blame game and excuses to try to end the relationship so they can begin the search for a new partner to restart all the thrills again.

Choosing a partner through instincts pure love between couples and abstaining from sexual desires at least in the first year of a relationship, will provide the opportunity for a true relationship to develop.

Moreover, when you become aware that your ego and instinct thoughts have the same level of desire for that person, you will find that, that level of desire does not diminish for the rest of your entire life.

Over this same period of time we have also witnessed the out of control freedom of the ego development of children as each generation relinquishes their responsibilities as parents more and more to the point where the children control the parents in many families.

This results in creating a life style for these people who when reaching adulthood struggle to cope with the demands of their ego and the attitude of other adults. Learning to listen to instinct is their only road to a more peaceful life but a difficult road.

One of the sadder issues of a permissive society is that when children are born to couples while they are still infatuated with their sexual desire for each other, then when it subsides and they go their separate ways, the children are the ones confused and receiving mixed messages about love.

The difficulty for all concerned is, that after separating from their ex-partners and becoming engaged in new relationships, the children from their previous relationship in many cases creates friction between all parties involved through one of egos learned creations "jealousy." In many circumstances this leads to another distorted view of what love is by all those involved, often because of another ego creation "hate."

It is critical that children have physically and emotionally affectionate parents or guardians during their formative years. For children whose carers are distant and cold or moving from one relationship to another, can themselves grow up to be needy, depressed adults and pursuing those same high sexual pleasures as being love.

The first obligation as an adult in a relationship when children are involved, must always be in the best interest of the children, and this philosophy needs to be applied to any partnership, at least until those children have reached an age where they are mature enough to understand the concept of love for themselves.

Mind you there are cases where a couple who have stayed together for the sake of the children, found that by the time the children were mature enough to understand, that the couple had actually grown to love each other as people not just as sexual partners.

Another issue to recognise in children is their desire of needing to be the best at everything they do. It may commence as sibling rivalry for attention from one or both parents, or by over competitive parents. If left unchecked develops into different forms of jealousy, even hate, depriving the children of a healthy sibling or friendship bond.

Often this extends into adulthood and acted out in similar behavior on work colleagues or sporting opponents. The person who has developed this type of ego requires a lot of nurturing from instinct.

Failures through any of ego innovations, desires and limited successes, even in non-competitive activities are the biggest letdown for ego and reverts to instinct for solitude and comfort, which instinct is always prepared to give.

One of the real dangers in self-love is the development of extreme negative thoughts by an ego-controlled mind, with the resulting outcome ending up as depression.

If it remains unchecked allowing ego to become obsessed to the point where no resolution is foreseeable and ignoring all reasoning from instinct completely, they then choose to terminate their own existence.

It is critical to acknowledge any signs of feeling unexplainable grief, firstly to your ego and instinct to work through, then to professional help when problems seem unsolvable, especially with issues that would not have been a bother to you previously.

ANGER

Generally the first response ego has to any failure or personal pain and commences very early in childhood, it can be the first notable signs of a persons' ego characteristics where things like impatience and temper can be observed, even as early as the tantrums of a demanding child wanting to be given attention.

Unfortunately, one of the common mistakes a parent makes is; by not responding to the child's needs, before it reaches the stage where the infant is crying loudly. The behaviour rewarded by providing the request from the angry actions displayed, establishing their ego belief that this is the best method to achieve the outcome desired.

The worst scenario as an adult from the development of this style of parenting following a lifetime of stress and frustration whenever life does not respond the way they want, as it most certainly will from time to time. May in a fit of uncontrollable rage inflict harm to him or herself, or if completely frustrated harm another person.

It is important to learn the difference between instinct anger, which is an assertive anger, and ego anger, which is an aggressive anger.

FEAR

Just as rewarding bad behavior from a child's angry responses can create a demanding ego, parents who respond with anger to a child's faults or failures can create an ego that responds to life's situations in fear. They are afraid of failure, always standing back, not getting involved, and difficulty accepting negative responses or results. The worst scenario for this style of behaviour is becoming very disillusioned with life; producing similar results as anger.

Learned fear behaviours from the ego provide the conditions necessary to make life difficult for some people particularly for those with a tendency to exaggerate the negative issues in their life.

Often these fears are potential at best but have the ability to cause the deterioration in health of the sufferer and make life a stressful journey. For some people sleep deprivation and stress are their constant companions trying to resolve not only their problems but the worlds as well.

It is important to recognise that instinct based fear is on achieving a positive outcome when in actual life threatened conditions, whereas ego based fears create if the thought of achieving a negative outcome is possible or by creating imaginary "scary" or phobic conditions, the ego has conjured up in its thoughts.

INTUITION

The issue here is overcoming the egos need to be right and in control, that has resulted in the inability for the majority of people in today's society to recognise intuition. Ego is louder than instinct and through fear or anger, able to override the intuitive feelings and thoughts that our emotive sense expresses which generally for most people has resulted in them ignoring their intuition, sometimes to their detriment when those thoughts were related to personal issues.

An interesting observation is though ego does not accept intuition or telepathy it does believe it has the ability to know what other people think, especially when ego believes that thought is negative or positive about them self.

An ego-controlled person has little difficulty in conjuring up an argument in their head over a perceived issue, often with no rationality to their argument or just as easily place them self on a pedestal as being well liked. They also know your needs, how many people are there in your life that knows what is best for you? The types of advice you receive from ego folk are generally something they just knew you needed or those times they did something for you without you asking because they knew you wanted it done.

JOY

The issue that ego has to overcome is in understanding the difference of experiencing joy with its own learned condition of happiness. It is common to hear people comment that they were happy that a person whom they did not like experienced some misfortune in their life, or that they will not be happy until they own a house, car, etc. Joy is never achievable from the result of a negative action or thought of the self or others in fact, achieving the opposite effect creating the condition of grief.

One in particularly is humour where both ego and instinct can be present if it is creating a positive mood. However, there are many degrees in differences when it comes to a persons' ego level of humour, and what may seem funny to some people is not always funny to others.

The problem is that in an ego controlled person, they often ignore the concerns for the feelings of others, resulting in causing embarrassment or even harm to others through what they had deemed to be as funny. Often people with this type of ego have little tolerance when the direction of the humour is at them. The reasoning instinct must put to ego when the humour appears offensive or harmful is "Would ego accept the humour being portrayed to be played on it if not then please stop."

GRIEF

As stated earlier more often than not, instinct has to come to the rescue of a grief stricken ego whose thoughts have become over absorbed in their loss. The issues here are recognising and coming to terms with, egos difficulty with losing conditions where it felt safe and comfortable, the inability to accept change and its obsession with any possessions it considers as its own.

A serious condition that parents who divorce should be aware of and negate quickly, is the level of grieving that a child engages in when they separate. Because for some children that grief becomes self-blame, where they bottle it up and it festers right through to adulthood. These same people then have difficulty with having a healthy relationship of their own not wanting to experience that level of pain again.

Another difficult issue that ego must learn to control when in a state of grief is "revenge" wanting to hurt someone else for the pain he or she is experiencing and inflicting similar feelings of loss to his or her accused in the belief that this will alleviate their pain. Often this revenge is in the form of verbal abuse with hurtful words that in most cases are untrue costing many relationships especially amongst family.

CHARACTER

One of today's hazards for child development is allowing children the freedom to create their own ego with parents and education systems failing to guide a child through all the instinct behaviours to create a balanced persona.

Instead, allowing him or her to over develop their strongest ego feature, resulting in the child being very focused on one-behaviour be it self-love, aggression, fearful, stressful, withdrawn, etc., which once developed, becomes a learned part of the character of that child. The behaviour may be tolerable when they are children however; there is not the same acceptance for that behaviour as an adult.

You may have already realised that this emotion also influences all the other six types of emotion in one form or another, and this will become more evident as we progress through both stages of being the person you were born to be.

Still as already stated, retraining ego to accept any change to its current thought patterns will be no easy task. No two people have exactly the same view on what is the required standard for a person's character; it will be up to each individual to decide when they know that they are the person, they were born to be.

STAGE 1

CHAPTER 7

RAISING INSTINCT PROFILE

I f you are starting to get that uncomfortable feeling that you're about to read about a journey into the make believe, don't worry, ego is reacting the only way it knows how, especially when it comes to accepting that your instinct is being allowed to participate in your decision making.

Probably your first hurdle is actually calming the random thoughts of the ego at least enough so that it becomes aware of the thoughts of instinct which are also always present, just not as loud.

This does not require a meditative state; it is simply a matter of not holding on to thoughts involving a plan, judgment, idea or a proposed conversation for this is ego at work, particularly those thoughts that keep repeating in various formats.

After a while, those thoughts will slow down enough so that you will begin to notice the surroundings and the sounds going on around you, this is instinct in action, observing your environment continuously. Of course, the more pleasant and safe your surroundings to allow ego becoming calm and relaxed the easier it will be to notice your instincts thoughts.

There are those who consider this as meditation; to me it is the first step to getting to know the complete you. I believe that meditation requires both ego and instinct to be calmed beyond thought because like ego, instinct is thinking all the time, in fact even when ego is sleeping. Therefore, in my mind accepting your complete self is something I consider as a compulsory requirement, whereas meditation is an activity of personal choice.

The term "baby steps" is extremely important when convincing ego that it will achieve much more in life if it takes instinct on board. It would be futile to begin to try to quiet the ego in the midst of a major decision you have been working through, it is much better to pick your battlegrounds and continue to bring instinct forward in calmer conditions.

If ego is not conjuring up conversations it would like to have or should have had, then it is planning some idea for the future or rehashing some event from the past, whereas instinct remains focused on what is happening now within the body and the body's surroundings.

To assist ego's thoughts to focus on now, will require ego to focus thoughts on either your body or the surroundings as well.

There are areas when instinct seems to be at its strongest, and ego is content to relax a little even if only for a short span, and these are generally when the effects of what we call "nature's beauty" is at its best. Some of these conditions include such things as; beaches, mountains, sunsets, etc.

Of course, one of the easiest ways to obtain unification of the thoughts without even the need to leave home is through the gift of music. If the music your ego bases its preference on requires negative or angry lyrics, it may require you to find a suitable alternative of instrumental music so that both achieve the same level of enjoyment.

The aim is that by providing conditions where agreement is easily achievable, eventually ego will become more aware of instinct thoughts until you sense the degree of acceptance entering into your ego thoughts. Gradually as you become more apt in the skill of involving the pair then it is possible to bring in other calming activities.

A common body one is the practice of focusing on your breathing and letting all ego thoughts dissipate allowing the presence of instinct thoughts heard.

I personally prefer a prolonged intake of each breath imagining it is penetrating all of my body during my inhale, or to a specific area of my body then as I am exhaling, any toxicity in my body exhales as well. This produces an imaginary result but it is one my instinct enjoys and ego seems to accept, because my ego thoughts also become calmer and more aware to the surroundings.

I have also noticed that my ego thoughts remain relaxed longer and those thoughts are in agreement with instinct. In time, you will find it easier to calm egos thoughts, as your instinct thoughts become more apparent, which enables you to attain a sense of wellbeing much more often.

Meditation is an important daily function for establishing calmness of your body and mind, mornings are the preferred time for me when my ego responds best and the practice I have discovered that assists me is:

Firstly, it is important that I endeavor to wake each day naturally, i.e. preferably without the aid of an alarm. The average person needs eight hours sleep per night and I aim to set my sleep period hours based on that fact.

Secondly, when my waking thought is bathroom, I complete that task and get back into bed. This action is also the option for me as well when I have to use an alarm because I need ego and instinct to be relaxed and at the forefront.

Thirdly, I lie on my back and join the opposing fingertips of the right and left hand together with my elbows resting at my sides. Then I focus on the contact points of those fingers until all thoughts dissipate.

While in this state, I experience a very light tingling sensation that starts from the finger tips then gradually over the entire body, a feeling similar to a small electrical current, which I assume, is the static electricity throughout my body that the emotive sense uses to communicate.

Once I move past this sensation, there is complete calm and silence, I spend as much time in this state as I can without it interfering with the requirements for exercising, dressing and having a healthy breakfast and I start my day stress free.

Be mindful that time takes on a different meaning in this meditative state for what seems like a few minutes can actually be 10-15 minutes before your instinct kicks into action again usually from an outer sound. You then need to go through the procedure again if you want to meditate longer.

The opportunity to spend time outdoors as part of your morning or evening ritual whether walking, jogging, riding or driving along your favourite spot always calms the ego allowing instinct to become involved in the thoughts of the surroundings.

Including activities involving the natural sounds of the area such as determining the variety of bird and animal sounds you can hear, the rhythm of the waves pounding on the beach, the breeze through the trees, etc. Are the types of things instinct focuses on that ego will also learn to enjoy if it appears as a challenge to identify?

Consuming your meals is a good avenue to bring the pair into discussion, particularly if you can eat outdoors for your meals. The emotive sense reports all the information from your taste buds of the flavours consumed to the brain, but unless it contains high amounts of sugar, salt or spices ego's thoughts are bored.

Turn the television off, put the newspaper or book away and sit outdoors, teach your ego to experience what the instinct is by enjoying every mouthful of food consumed.

Learning the variety of tastes in each vegetable and fruit is something the ego will pursue especially if it is a challenge against the instinct and purchasing a wide variety of each to enhance that challenge is better for your health.

Many of the decisions you make in your life are by your instinct. One of the main reasons for this is that instinct knows your capabilities and limitations, and because ego wants to operate in the fast lane, pursuing the maximum life can offer, which at times is more than the body's capabilities.

When it cannot attain the result it desires, ego creates excessive stress levels within the body and instinct is required to calm ego and take control of the situation.

Averting many of these situations was possible if ego and instinct had been working as a team from the beginning. Because any idea or plan that ego perceives as a rewarding one has to include instinct if it is to succeed.

If you stop and consider the number of ideas or schemes your ego has come up with in your life to make you successful, rich or admired, how many even got further than an idea or at best a passing phase.

For me the truth is that any results you have actually achieved was due to the involvement of your instinct also having the desire to achieve that idea. Most tasks, once learned become routine and the duty of instincts recall to perform, while ego plans and schemes new and exciting ideas.

Anyone who drives a car on an extended routine trip will have experienced daydreaming of some plan or idea for the future and suddenly becoming aware that you cannot recall having passed through the last town. Other activities such as the ability to swim, ride a bike or ski to name a few become the responsibility of instinct to recall.

In many instances, instinct through the emotive sense provided you with the feelings of satisfaction acquired in the achievements gained through each task, on the way to completing the goal.

While your ego was in the background, focused mainly on reaching the completion of this goal or what actions are needed to make you more successful or so that it could start a new and better project.

Your goal therefore, is to make ego accept how important instinct is to your daily life that it must be involved in your daily thoughts, which is attainable through regular breathing and meditation practices or Yoga techniques all in suitable surroundings as discussed, continually keeping the ego in a stress free zone where possible.

The realisation will be apparent when you feel that the issues raised previously between the two have dissipated and that you are rationalising many of your thoughts more than previously.

What is important at this point is that you have kept this program as yours alone. That you have not involved anyone else to observe your progress or even have expectations that people will notice any changes in you. Too many people try to do things just so it will bring recognition or attention to them, a trait you now know as one of egos.

CHAPTER 8

INSTINCT
AND YOUR HEALTH

Continuing the baby step approach, the next steps are to
make the ego appreciate everything about itself.

It becomes easier to recognise the control the ego has over
your thoughts in most activities you engage in, particularly when
exerting physical energy that you would not normally do.

Your organs or other parts of the body will commence sending
messages via the emotive sense to the brain that this exertion is
beyond the normal standards usually expected of them to perform
so "please stop now".

If the ego is responding to a challenge, it will force the body
to continue. This will often produce results that will please the
ego, particularly when sporting activities are involved or you are
trying to improve your body shape or impress someone.

Unfortunately, when it is forcing parts of the body to perform
to levels beyond its normal capabilities or that they are not healthy
or fit enough to cope with, that is when unnecessary damage to
the body results.

The numbers of broken bones hospitals attend to daily are uncountable, in many instances, the damage may only result in a strained muscle, but if that muscle is in the heart then you may not get the chance to pay more attention to those messages in the future.

Blame is a favorite tool of the ego, when perceiving anything as a failure ego is very quick to nominate where responsibility lies, unless of course it is with itself.

However, if other sources are not to be found, then some people will be heard saying "I blame myself for being so stupid" or "I could kick myself" but are they really blaming their ego self.

In truth, the ego will in fact be blaming the instinct for not being more assertive during the discussion stage when ego dismissed the reasons put forward by instinct warning that the plan or activity was flawed. Particularly when an injury to the body has resulted from the actions taken, or likewise, resulted in embarrassment incurred to ego.

Have you ever noticed when visiting your doctor because you are not feeling well, they will always start with "and what seems to be the problem" So you proceed to explain all the symptoms that your body is telling you, then the doctor checks to see if those symptoms are valid to determine a diagnoses.

In many situations, you already know the diagnoses, and you are only seeking the authority necessary to obtain the healing medicine. The truth is that instinct is communicating with your entire body 24/7 and you need to retrain ego to be more receptive to the information.

In previous chapters, we discussed examples of when the instinct is sensing danger, desire, trust, etc. However, it is also telling you just how healthy your body is at any given moment, also what is required to repair any deficiencies.

Most people are aware of intestinal issues from over-eating fatty or exotic foods, just as we know when the persistent cough starts first thing every morning, that those cigarettes are damaging the lungs. When checking the time to see if it is OK to take that first alcoholic drink for the day, that the alcohol is taking control over the body.

However, what about all the subtle signs you can observe, such as dull or hazy eyes, cracked or brittle nails, dry or blotchy skin, split or breaking hair, urine color, stool composition, always tired or lack of libido. In fact, every itch and twitch, pang or twang, ache or pain is your body's way of communicating that attention is required and there is an indicator for almost every fault, which unfortunately the ego tends to overlook.

If instinct were in total control, then it would address these messages immediately. However, because ego is the more demanding, then it will want to ignore these signs and continue to indulge in whatever activity it is involved with at that time. The problem is that as far as ego is concerned that when there is a health issue concerning the body, that it has access to medical help to bring the problem under control and remedy the situation at a time that is more convenient.

Unfortunately, that time often does not occur until it no longer is enjoying the results received from the activity, by then you have already inflicted the damage to your body. The opposite scenario for some is when ego ignores any health problems because it is thinking in the negative, that each issue with health is fatal, and is either a form of cancer or heart disease. In addition, because of egos fear of death it arouses your sense of fear, which results in the irrational thoughts that produce unnecessary stress.

I am certain that everyone knows someone who refuses to have a cancer check, heart check or regular medical check simply because "they would rather not know" Unfortunately, these same people spend most of their waking day living in a state of anxiety, while at the same time doing very little to give their body the opportunity to be healthy.

When ego gets into this condition it is then up to instinct to calm the situation to reduce the fear built up in your body, which in fact is damaging your body through unnecessary stress levels to conditions existing totally in your ego thoughts. Those thoughts in the background trying to relax the ego mood is instinct at work.

Learn to listen to the thoughts, read the signs that your instinct is projecting when the body is in stress or tired, while ego is still pushing to achieve. Although they will not be loud, thoughts of "moderation" will be constantly interjecting, if ignored by ego can result in harm to the body.

The problem is that everything comes at a price, especially once the body gets "out of whack" becoming fatigued through lack of sleep or proper diet. Then loss of motivation sets in and egos enthusiasm begins to wane, becoming another failed activity or project.

Instead of continuing until the damage has resulted, a better outcome is to let instinct participate in the journey. This then gives you the opportunity to pace yourself and create a better balance in your life. Teaching ego the art of moderation in all aspects of your life will be the challenge for instinct, nonetheless one achievable.

Balance is the real key to looking after your body with what you eat and drink, everything you consume, provided it be in proportion to your size will not render you overweight. Listening to your emotive sense when the stomach organ informs that it has had enough to eat or drink is that key, which is generally a heavy sigh.

Of course, the more natural foods and fluids you consume are, the better your health will be, but if food has to be in a package then try to keep it supplied frozen fresh where possible.

Movement is also essential for a balanced healthy body; for the average person this does not require you to engage in extreme fitness activities or even extended workouts that ego suggests.

The saying "use it or lose it" needs to be your gauge, that means at least moving all the parts of your body that you can move on a daily basis at an increased heart rate, particularly those areas of the body that do not form part of your routine activities.

In order to have the energy to live an active life you need to provide your body with the right ingredients and maintenance programs, which as an added bonus also provides the ability to live longer while maintaining your health.

CHAPTER 9

EGO WITH OTHER BEINGS

At this point, I feel the need to stress that though nature is very pleasing to observe or be actively involved with both for instinct and the ego, it is critical that we give nature the respect it deserves.

There are far too many lives lost unnecessarily through their flippant attitude toward nature and the power or forces it has, particularly when challenging the ocean, river, floods, bush fires, etc. never mind those who challenge nature by living in areas that regularly encounter earthquakes, hurricanes, tornadoes, volcanic eruptions, etc.

While many of these phenomena's are also beautiful to observe in their own right, it is a tragedy and waste of life when human beings take on nature for any reason, especially if allowing ego to dominate their decision and ignoring all the warning systems of their instinct.

The unfortunate decision for many of these deaths is that the victims have confidence in their religious beliefs, and that because of those beliefs this will somehow protect them from harm by any of nature's fury.

This next step in the process of training the ego to see the things instinct sees is in the areas of the environment and the animals.

As I expressed earlier if there is one thing that brings ego and instinct into agreement it is beauty, in particular, natural beauty. During the early stages of this journey the more you involve yourself in observing natural beauty, the more you will find that the two will spend more time in agreement.

A visit to your nearest Planetarium will provide you with the opportunity to witness god's work in controlling and maintaining the universe. The most awesome views you will ever encounter are those areas of the universe that we are able to see. From the distinguishing colours and size of each planet in our solar system, to the magnificence of the colours and sizes of other star systems in our galaxy indeed, the patterns and structures of other galaxies.

In addition, the realisation of how small our planet is, and the insignificance our own existence is in terms of the universe. That whatever you achieve in your life cycle in reality is for your own peace of mind that you were worth something as a person.

Some of the beauty that this planet has to offer, for the majority of people will always be a dream, that if they ever win a lot of money they would spend their lives getting to see all those magnificent creations on our planet. Places such as the Grand Canyon, Victoria Falls, Swiss Alps, Andes Mountains to name a few.

However, it does not have to be a dream, nor does it; require a lot of money to experience some of the magnificent views that exist in your own country, state or even in your district. Although not on as grand a scale, there are many beautiful mountains, canyons, gorges, waterfalls, etc. that certainly measure up as natural beauty.

These days many local government bodies have turned their special nature features into tourist attractions, such as lookouts or viewing platforms, picnic areas, walking tracks, etc to attract the tourist dollar.

I am certain there are those of you who are saying right now that nothing worth looking at exists in your district. However, let me ask this, do you have a botanical garden, are there flower shows, walking/bike paths, have you ever just walked the streets in your town observing the garden displays of your neighbors.

I must admit that for many years, I ignored these and many other activities that enabled me to observe the enormous array of plant life that exists on this planet. In fact, botanists still do not have a full listing of every plant existing on earth.

I now believe that when it comes to the individual identification of a plant that it is likely that each has their own special unique markings providing the magnificent varieties of colours, textures and durability of each species of plant that is unobserved by most humans just as each of the animal species has their own unique markings.

Take a walk outside to the nearest tree and observe its structure, how it is designed to withstand the climate conditions, the colours that are present just in your vision. At first glance, you may only observe a brown trunk and branches with green leaves; if you study it much closer you will be amazed at the many different colours present.

Do not be surprised if you discover that your ego is quite intrigued by this activity and in many cases prepared to explore further. Until like me visiting botanical gardens when travelling becomes a normal inclusion to the journey. You might consider attending the local flower shows or annual shows where people display the results from caring for a plant, fruit or vegetable from conception to full fruition some people create amazing results.

It is understandable that the majority of people get some enjoyment out of observing animals especially those in their natural environment. Thus, the popularity of documentaries on wildlife films because for many people the opportunity only is available through this medium. What is more unfortunate is that for many species they are now only visible in zoos or aquariums because they are almost extinct.

Again as with plant life, have you ever taken the time to observe the many varieties of animals that exist in your country, state district or yard? Take a walk around the lake, along the river, stream, creek or parkland then sit and observe, you will be quite surprised at the variety of animal life in your district particularly birdlife.

In fact, you do not need to venture very far from your own back door to discover an abundance of life. The variety of insects, spiders, bugs snails, lizards, mice, etc. all live in their own world oblivious to everything except their own survival.

The observation that I found incredible was the realisation of the interconnection between the plant life and animal life, how one is dependent on the other. For in all situations nature had provided the plant or animal with the necessities to sustain their existence either through other plants or through other animals, also the realisation that human beings were somewhere in that category.

Once this interconnection becomes obvious, it is impossible to ignore the fact that we as human beings are destroying too much of the plant and animal life. That if we do not stop, the time will come when we will in fact place our own existence in jeopardy from the gaps we are creating in the food chain.

Any of these suggestions for looking or listening are a tool to retrain both the ego and the instinct and you may have a whole other list of activities that your character would respond better.

In fact, any system that allows your ego and instinct to become a team in your behaviour pattern should be encouraged, especially with regard to listening, looking and learning about your true self.

If there is only one thing that you receive from participation in this segment, I hope is the realisation that all beings are on this earth for a purpose. Humans are yet to understand what those purposes are for many beings and the question to ask is do we need to, instead just accept the fact that they are.

CHAPTER 10

YOUR TRUE CHARACTER

During our formative year's ego is quite strong and controlling, and it is common to see children refusing to share, acting cruelly towards other children or defiant towards authority.

Depending on the reasoning power of instinct we "grow out of it" by the time we reach adulthood. Unfortunately, one of the down sides of our modern society is that many people are retaining many of those childhood behaviour patterns into adulthood.

Accepting the negative behaviours that you have had for as long as you can remember is your first task, as these will be the hardest ones for you to change and it may be easier to tackle other areas first.

Moreover, now that ego is on board and working as a team or at least listening to instinct's thoughts, then there is an opportunity to make peaceful negotiations in any of the areas of your life that "you know in the back of your mind" could be or need to be, done better.

This is the area where you bring into play instincts emotive sense in the role of character. It is also here where the virtue of "understanding" assists ego to accept that the instinct emotions instantly felt throughout the body include the brain, of which it is a part.

Instinct will need to provide examples constantly, demonstrating that when the response of the body reacts immediately, it is due to the emotive sense receiving data from the physical senses or the organs. This includes the fact that ego also uses the emotive sense unknowingly to transmit its alternate emotions.

The adrenalin rush that untold numbers of people experience daily from the many activities such as fun parks, extreme sports, etc. that the ego knows is safe and considers as fun, but sends fear reactions from the instinct are prime examples.

The next area to concentrate your focus is that you are living in an ethical manner. Your "ethics" are the rules of conduct that make you the individual you are and how your actions will provide you with the right peace of mind.

One of the greater tools that instinct has is the power of reasoning; we have all seen those cartoons with the little devil on one shoulder encouraging evil acts, while on the opposite shoulder the little angel pleads for goodness.

This scenario is required when the ego goes into the role of being "judgmental." It is up to the instinct to speak louder and teach the ego to be more "flexible" and show more "compassion" towards others and the self.

However, it is not your level of ethics that are achievable to be "judging" yourself based on the level that others live, accepting that their level is "good enough" that will contribute to you being the person you were born to be.

Similarly, neither is your standard of ethics achieved by judging others on the expectations your ego has set for them, that you are not applying to yourself. For it is actually the opposite in that you prefer other people to want to live to the high standards that you live.

Ego must learn to depend less on assumptions, and instead, directly on actual experiences as the true guide. For example, once having experienced a healthy body, it will "know" when that condition is changing and to listen to instinct to the needs for correction.

The same applies to the instinct; once having experienced the calm in a peaceful life then it is easier for instinct to recognise when ego is heading in the wrong direction and be more "diligent" to negotiate with ego.

By being a person of "integrity" and doing what you say you will do, will have an impact on all the virtues of character, for only those who live to their highest values and virtues are living a life of integrity. Have you promised to do something and did not, or did the opposite with seemingly no remorse?

Do you consider yourself as someone who is "reliable" "truthful" in your relationships with your partner, family, and your friends? What could you do better? How often have you "let down" or disappointed the ones you love?

How do you rate yourself in terms of being "trustworthy?" Are you "honest" in your personal and business dealings with others and treat everyone fair in fact, are you "honest" with yourself and accept your limitations.

Do you show "respect" for self and others treating everyone equally and as equals, in order for you to "honour" yourself as a person, you need to be able to "respect" yourself as a person before you can respect others.

It requires instinct to maintain a constant focus on the thoughts of the ego to teach those concepts of "consideration" for self and others, of "courteousness" performing acts of "decency" and demonstrating the "gentler" side of your character.

Once you start showing acts of "kindness" and be more "caring" toward yourself and others, you will notice the calmness and feelings of general well being in your body and mind.

Although I have not mentioned every virtue I listed in Part Two under the heading of character, I am confident that from the examples just given that you will indeed review each one to confirm that each is a part of your thinking.

It is important to remember to detach yourself from receiving rewards for these acts especially that of recognition by others.

In addition, while monetary and material donations to charity organizations are to be encouraged; these are not the actions to accept as "doing your bit".

The next step is to get instinct to listen and respond to ego's creative thoughts that give you the opportunity to improve those standards. If you do not involve egos enthusiasm to succeed, you will definitely not get egos commitment.

You only achieve all the virtues of your character through keeping your ego thoughts calm, listening to the input from instincts thoughts, reaching an agreement and then acting on them. Because it is here that, you will find the person you were born to be and that person is the one who performs to the standards you were born with to achieve in all areas of the character sense.

Nonetheless, it will require the desire of the ego and the ability of instinct to achieve it. The ability to separate the two thoughts will require constant attention, for ego will still push the boundaries even for such things as acts of kindness, generosity, courtesy, etc.

At this stage, you are fully aware of your ego behaviour patterns moreover, you now have the ability to recognise those controlling types of thoughts, which ego still will, even while in the pursuit of being the person you were born to be. It is critical to know when ego has taken over your thoughts and instinct is simply complying, usually that point occurs when you find that you are becoming obsessed about obtaining a result and other thoughts consumed with how you have become such a better person.

The moment those thoughts commence occurring, stop whatever you are doing, calm the ego thoughts so the instinct can respond on how it feels the direction is heading, specifically with meeting the need to fulfill the appropriate virtues that are now a part of your new character. That response will enable self-discipline of your behaviour, so that ego and instinct listen, then appraise their thoughts for the best actions before proceeding any further.

Now is the time to review your original notes from earlier in the book and the long-term behaviours you identified at the beginning of this chapter. My hope is that your behaviour patterns are now different; nonetheless, it is a good opportunity to see what you are thinking now and if any other areas of improvements are possible.

There will be friends and family members that believe "you have gone soft in your old age" These same people may distance themselves from your circle when struggling to accept the changes in your behaviour, which is OK, for you no longer need the approval of others. What you will find is the people now moving into your life are of similar character enhancing your peaceful existence.

To have the freedom to enjoy the world that you are a part of without placing limitations for fear of embarrassment provides you the chance to experience life as it should be experienced.

Enjoy the outdoors and all it offers as much as you can, relax with family and friends; enjoy time alone meditating or any exercise discussed and be the person you were born to be.

This concludes stage one and I hope you gained enough information to enable you to make the necessary adjustments to your previous way of life that placed any restrictions on how you live.

STAGE 2

CHAPTER 11

DOING WHAT YOU WERE BORN TO DO

At this point, you have not only recognised all your ego and instinct traits. Moreover, made the necessary changes that is providing you with a new inner peace along with an appreciation of the ways humankind behave in the manner that they do.

Armed with all this new knowledge and perception you now need to decide what it is you really want for yourself. Is your family life complete, do you have a satisfying career, are you content with your social life.

For simplifying the process, I want to use the methodology to pursue your career life, as this in most cases has an impact on both the family and social life or if you are now commencing out in life in search of a career.

If you are content with your career then it may prove fruitful to use the following method to broaden other areas of your life's goals or to include your family and friends more into your life.

For a majority of people be it through good fortune, intuition or a knowing from early childhood, are in fact content with the careers they have chosen. For others it is all about watching the clock continuously, desperate for their next break or end of shift with no joy in their work in fact, wishing their life away. Cheating them of living a life where their time spent, is the most important priority to have for a life of contentment.

Others move from job to job with money being the only criteria to work. Money, as a goal is never achievable because you adjust to the level of your income no matter what level of income reached and then you need more or become greedy and want more. You may feel cheated because you find enough time is not available for you to maintain a balance of work, family and play. Whatever the reason is only you can change your life.

What I am proposing now is a systematic plan that will provide you with the opportunity to make the necessary changes to your current life to do what you were born to be doing and live the life that in reality you want to live.

Some of you are already wincing because you see it may require starting at the beginning of a completely new career while still having to maintain your current work life. This will require perseverance on your part and that requires belief in the goal you want to achieve.

STEP 1: GETTING STARTED

The first step is the decision to make a start, and in doing so be realistic. For example, there is not much point in wanting to pursue a career as a professional football star at 40 years of age. However, that does not mean you should deny yourself the opportunity to be involved in the game you love and breathe every day. There are many fields to become involved in, such as coaching, training, marketing, health to name a few, that can provide you with a life of involvement and income in the very thing you love.

There will be no short cuts, and it will likely take longer to complete any new career than you anticipated, mostly you will need to be committed or the result will not be forth coming. The big difference here will be that you are involved in doing something you were born to do. A clue to success is not putting too much pressure on you. Instead, enjoy the journey and the time it takes to achieve the goal.

You need to take that first step to get started, because it is not possible to have the career you were born to perform until you do. While ever you are lamenting about the could be's, the should be's or the want to be's you are not being true to yourself, it is time to give you the chance to live the life you were born to live. So take that first step.

STEP 2: CAREER SELECTION

The second step is determining exactly what you were born to do. I have already written that the makeup of our DNA and genes provides us with certain skills, talents and learning abilities in certain fields than others.

There is always the case where individuals have succeeded, particularly in sporting careers despite their shape or size. Those people have managed to defy the norm overcoming those obstacles through pure determination knowing what they were born to do and doing it.

The education level, family, peers or social environment governs far too many people's lives preventing any inkling of a career of choice often from an early age. To find that career requires a journey to the inner self, getting your instinct involved your ego under control and opening the mind to what you really enjoy.

Are you an indoor or outdoor person, do you enjoy working with your hands, computers, music, art, etc. What is it that you do well or interests you more than anything else interests. Moreover, if so what career fields are possible for you to pursue.

Obviously, you will have more than one choice in the beginning; still I hope you take the opportunity to listen to your intuition, as it will keep coming back to that one particular choice that will be your final preference.

Sometimes there are people who may be unaware of their talent, especially if their lifestyle has not enabled them any involvement with their talent to date in their life. For example, if after completing your education you accepted the first job offered to you and you were still in that job today, you may not recognise the special talents you actually possess.

In this circumstance, you need to let the thoughts flow in and out of your mind. Maybe you recall a desire you had during your adolescent years, is there a particular field that has held your interest, do you find it easy to perform specific handyman skills, do you have plans for a hobby when you retire, list all your thoughts dismiss nothing.

The list may seem large even daunting in the beginning and you will need to ensure that it is not ego controlled. Especially to those that point strongly to fame and fortune, even though your choice may indeed end up in a career that does provide you with that life, it is not the reason for this journey.

You also need to be practical, specifically that you are capable of earning a living in your choice. Money should not be at the top of the list in your choices but it needs to be an essential part of your decision if it is your career.

It is also important that you are not basing your choices on ease of completion resulting in a waste of time and effort for you, ending as another poor career choice.

Your instinct knows what you were born to do; there will be various telltale signs as you near the end of your search, so it is critical not to ignore any such body indicators or intuitive feelings.

Try not to reach a conclusion too quickly as to which field you want to work in once you decide what you believe is where you want to spend your career time.

For example, because you devote all your spare time working in your flower garden, decide you will pursue producing flowers as a career. If you step back and ask, what is it about the gardening that I really love? What is it that I do best? That I find gives me the most satisfaction. Maybe it is not the production of the flowers, but the landscaping results that you produce and the flowers are merely part of the overall result you achieve.

The added bonus from this particular example as with any hobby you love; is that you would be spending your career time doing what you were doing in your leisure time. Now your leisure time becomes available to spend on other things, such as your family and friends or other relaxing social activities.

For a variety of people, they may take the view that they have reasonable job satisfaction already and earn a good living doing it. Preferring to continue to do what they love doing as a hobby, devoting their free time to that hobby. To those people I say, it is your life and you are entitled to live it how you see it. Some things you might like to consider though

Are the "other people" in your life just as content, do you still fit in regular outings with the family, do you help your children with their homework, and do you eat meals as a family?

By keeping your passion and your work separate, are you managing to provide quality time into the five key areas equally. Namely family, work, hobby, sleep and have a social life as well. Which of the five areas is first to suffer or are all areas in truth being treated below the standard you would prefer.

Being content with all aspects of your life is a juggling act and the more balls you have to juggle the harder it is to maintain that balance of contentment. So if it is possible to reduce the key areas of your life from five to four, where your work and sleep hours remained the same opening the door to a much larger family and social life, should you not at least consider the choice.

There are hobbies considered unusable as a career, because they cannot provide a livable wage, you will need to determine if there are career paths associated with your hobby that do provide that wage such as a hobby shop or continue to balance your life now with six possible areas during the transition phase if you pursue a new career.

The long-term gain may be to suspend your hobby in favour of pursuing that career, particularly if that hobby is not time based.

As the overall improvement to your life in the end could replace the time lost on your hobby.

STEP 3: PLAN DEVELOPMENT

The third step is to develop a plan, a systematic strategy to accomplish your goal of a new career you were born to do.

Firstly, you need to review the skills you already have achieved be it education, knowledge or practical skills you have attained to date and how you can take advantage of those achievements in the quest towards your new career.

Secondly, to determine the shortfalls that you have currently, that you will need to undertake to make your new goal viable. Be careful not to attempt engaging in short cuts or sub-standard methods, as the time and care you put into the preparation of your plan could result in the difference between succeeding and failing to achieve the goal.

Thirdly, it is also important that your plan include your current work, family and personal life, as it will require a fine balance of all these three to fit in with obtaining a new career. Unless there is a balanced approach, the risk of "burning out" will be a distinct possibility.

Fourthly, it is essential that you are enjoying the journey; remembering that ego is mainly goal focused so setting your plan to progress via small step tasks help to keep ego in control.

Impatience, frustration, lack of self-belief, listening to others, even comparing you to others is all the traits of the ego.

Instinct needs to come to the fore whenever these or other ego traits appear, ego needs constant reminding that it is OK to be uncertain even fearful where there is no guarantee of success.

Finally, your plan must also be dynamic as there will invariably be that unforeseen hurdle you have to detour around when you least expect it. A part of the challenge that you have undertaken, if you always keep in mind the journey is the plan, the experience is the reward.

One of the most challenging and rewarding dynamic changes you will face is if children come into your life from the moment of their conception until you depart this life.

In times gone by only the fathers missed the majority of the daily pleasures of witnessing their children's development. These days however, it is the daycare centre, preschool, prep school right through to high school that gets to be the owners of that joy, with the majority of women now needing to join the workforce.

The tragedy with this common scenario is that now the person your child was born to be, the machine that is conformity is instead developing their mannerisms, character, thoughts, skills, etc. the opportunity stolen from them to develop their natural talents and character as an individual.

That machine reprograms those talents and character to meet the group mentality behaviour, most likely to the standards and beliefs of the teachers in those establishments controlling their life. I know that school is compulsory and education is vital to survive in this world today however, every effort and sacrifice possible needs made as a parent during the formative years of children.

If you have children and are now in that process of redeveloping your life in the direction of being the person you were born to be. Ensure that within that plan you include providing your children with the opportunity to do the same, because the family must always be included in the priority list with everything you want to achieve.

STEP 4: TIME MANAGEMENT

The fourth step is time management, setting a timeframe for your plan to achieve your new career. In particular, if you needed to obtain new education qualifications or trade certificates which will not see you producing any results for years.

Other aspects to consider may be volunteering your time free of charge to obtain work experience in your chosen field, part time work, costs involved for equipment, tools of trade to be purchased; in fact any or all expenditures needs to be included in your time scaled plan.

Good time management means addressing the level of every decision made and prioritising it. Understanding the importance of how each decision affects the total time to complete the goal, enables you to afford the time and care to provide the solutions that add value to your project.

Beware of ego bogging down with sorting what are the main priorities and what are the surface issues, whenever ego shows signs of this behaviour, take a break, go for a walk and allow instinct to talk it through and calm ego down.

A calm mind is essential to setting out a workable time management program for the order you wish to attack your plan.

Otherwise, a lot of work may end up being lost or incomplete if overlooking a vital step or placing a step in the wrong sequence of progress for the project.

Just as you included your current work life, family and personal life in your plan for a new career, you will also need to do the same in your time management plan.

In particular, your family life as the truth is you cannot afford to give them any less time than you currently do or want to do. You will need their support and the support of your friends, if nothing else at least their understanding in what you are now endeavoring to achieve.

One of the many confronting obstacles you will discover the moment you begin planning your time management schedule will be how little free time you have available without consuming all your weekend.

In the perfect world of the standard 5-day week there are minimum hours already taken up, you are at work 40-50 hrs; you are sleeping 35-40 hrs; leaving you approximately 30-45 hrs of "free time" during the week. However, you still need to deduct meal times, travel time for work, family time, personal grooming, hygiene and exercise time and do not forget time to relax and just chill out.

It becomes apparent immediately that some activities have to go, and if you have a hobby that you love, that is where the chill out time or exercise time already disappeared to in all probability.

This will require putting in place any time saving feature that you can apply. Moreover, combining activities to free up any spare moment you can, directing that time to your new career plan.

For instance, ensuring that the family has breakfast and dinner together every day possible, you can discuss each member's activity plan for the day at breakfast, then what they achieved through the day at dinner.

The option of you using public transport for work travel time, so you can use that time to study or review your completed tasks or next steps. Maybe consider purchasing a bicycle or jogging to work in order to maintain an exercise in your program.

These days many companies allow their employees to stagger their work hours; do shift work or work from home that could reduce your travelling time and increase the family time. You will not know unless you ask and it may pay to be honest for your reasons for the request particularly if your new career has an opportunity within your company.

Be careful if you decide to reduce your sleep time. While there are many people that can perform at their peak with below the average of eight hours sleep a day, this should not be one of your first selections.

In fact, unless you are in that group of people who struggle to stay in bed for eight hours let alone sleep, then you should avoid this concept completely.

The last thing that any plan needs is one that will result in "Burn out". However, that is a guarantee for anyone who heads down the path of extended periods of sleep deprivation as his or her plan to create free time for the project.

The other area to be careful with is your time for relaxation or just chilling out. All work and no play can also result in "Burn out" so there will be a need for time in your weekly schedule to unwind.

In all probability, you will only have the luxury of a few hours a week and you will need to juggle those hours amongst your favourite activities in the monthly plan and most likely they will be all limited to weekends.

Maintaining balance in your life is the key to a successful journey towards your goal, and for some people quiet time alone in pleasant surroundings to meditate or pray works for them.

For others a romantic night out, attending a game of your favourite sport, a function with the family and/or friends, while it may appear a waste of time that you do not really have to spare, it is just as necessary as sleep for overall well being of the self.

How you spend your time to unwind only you can decide. It is critical however that you do provide that time in your schedule, this is a journey of change requiring your full attention and you can only achieve it if you are operating at your peak to reach your goal.

STEP 5: IMPLEMENTATION

The fifth step is putting the plan into action, remember the "KISS" principle (Keep It Simple Stupid) and complete the basic tasks first, ego will need positive results in the beginning to be enthusiastic.

A good method to apply is, when reaching each target have some form of reward in place such as a special dinner or a movie, may be both if the task was significant. Including the family and friends in any of those reward systems is an added bonus, as it will make them a part of your journey.

It is extremely important that these people fully support your journey, as they too will be required to make sacrifices with their time as well, along with their patience and understanding. Try to keep them informed so they have an appreciation of how and why you have progressed to each set target.

This journey requires you to remain positive at all times, therefore each task you set yourself needs to produce a result that is showing a positive step towards your completing the journey.

This requires a major change for anyone whose previous character had been one of negativity. You will need to have made the necessary changes to your character to be at this point, those negative behaviours recognised by you in the earlier chapters of this book.

You will find it difficult to trust your instinct in the early stages of this journey, moreover your intuition that has played a major role in your decision-making.

With time, you will develop respect for both and will rely on them more and more in your daily decisions. The respect you have for heights, water, fire, animals and insects to name a few integrated into your intellect at conception, as did what you were born to be and do.

Be aware that some people will move out of your life, as many people do not like change but new people more aligned with your new direction will replace these. Of course, some people will be prepared to disagree with your plan and/or timeframe, only to ready and willing to advise you of a better system.

It is at this time when ego and instinct need to make a stand as one, politely listen to their advice and thank them for their input, but unless it will actually improve your plan, stick with what you have already spent hours creating.

This is the time to remember that instinct will tend to go along with any ego decision in your method of progress, however allowing others to interfere and take control results in it no longer being your plan.

It may appear easier on the surface to accept the plan of someone already successful in completing the career path that you are now embarking on. However, beware that accepting the plans of others may be ego's way of providing itself with an excuse for failure, someone else to blame or accepting the easy road.

This is your journey and the mistakes and successes need to be yours alone, that is what will make it an enjoyable journey. Keep in mind at all times, that this is a life changing career plan for you. You were born with the capability to learn all the skills necessary to do this career; any influences from outside sources may cause your plan to fail.

When ego first digests the plan, it will see the possibilities of great success, unfortunately, when it sees the effort required to achieve the goal that is when the fear of failure will raise its ugly head. How successful you are is only a factor of how many limits you place on your potential.

By working through the adversities you will meet along the road to success and above your comfort zone, you may find that there are no actual limits to your potential and to what you can achieve. Each individual has his or her own opinion to what successful means, only you have the right to acknowledge when you feel you have reached that milestone as we are discussing your life.

The real secret of you achieving success is never give up; I read a quote once that stated, "If success was easy than everyone would be successful". Usually when we see or hear of someone being successful, we are only receiving the result of their end journey, we have no idea of the challenges and hardships they endured to get there.

Be prepared that as soon as it appears you are being successful that out of the woodwork come the negative people, those who suffer from the tall poppy syndrome. Do not fall for it; do not waste your time or energy trying to prove anything to these people or anyone else. Your outcomes are yours alone, the only proof you need is to yourself and that will be apparent just by the arrival of these types of people.

One of the difficult areas on this journey that most likely you will need to negotiate is coping with the needs of others in your life. There will be times when you will have to say "NO" in order for you to achieve success. Times when you will need to make your needs the top priority.

Before you reach the point, where you are earning a sufficient income in your new life career, you will have to juggle your time with your current life career. It is important that the others in your life understand what is important to you, what you have time for and what you do not.

It is equally important that you fully explain the reasons anytime you do say "NO". Particularly with your family, otherwise feelings of guilt on your part will result. Proper communication with everyone involved in your journey will help ease the many difficult times you will face on each occasion that you have to say "NO".

There will be a lot of pressure on you right throughout achieving your goal, but taking the time to explain, and often explaining repeatedly that helps to maintain your sanity and peace of mind.

Among many of the difficult situations you will face is "Letting go" of your current life. The reality is that many of the aspects of your life to date have been enjoyable, but not totally fulfilling.

That is why you are on this journey but that will mean, "Letting go" of many things that until now were of importance to you. You know to whom I am referring, yes your other half "ego" who will really struggle with this concept. For many people change is a difficult journey, for them it seems too hard to let go of what they already have worked hard to achieve. It will be important to establish a pace of change that you and your family are physically and mentally able to cope with personally.

Egos attachment to "things" such as way of life, reputation, other people, physical objects, etc. place limitations on your capacity to get the most out of life. Accepting the flow of life that "things" come and go and the attachment to them, releases restrictions on your ability to move on from your current life.

I am not suggesting that you become detached from everything in your life for a single moment. Instead, I am advocating you enjoy everything that is in your life at this moment, that moment is now and a continually changing one. Let your instinct override your ego and simply enjoy whatever you are experiencing in this present moment.

The person you were and the lifestyle you had, you wanted to be different from the moment you started reading this book and became aware of an ego-based life. Becoming aware that your instinct is the true guide of your life and making those necessary adjustments to your character has enabled you to be on the path you are on now. It also enables you to cope much better when you are under stress or pressure from your workload, providing you with the behavioural skills to handle those times when your plans do not go the way you intended.

Some of your plans will follow their natural course; however, some will not work out. That does not mean that you chose the wrong career, it means you need to either find another way to achieve your goal or redefine the goal. I touched on the need to change direction earlier; in fact, it may require you to quit the direction you are heading.

If for example, your heart desire is to be an actor then you will need to prepare yourself for a road that will be long and hard with rejection the norm. You will need to condition your thinking to the knowledge that there is no such thing as an "overnight success". Many actors do not get to taste the thrill of success despite them being in the game since their childhood, still waiting to land that leading role in a play, show or movie.

You may have enjoyed the successes of school plays then the local theatre club as an adult, especially if you were the best in your local group. Now, you are just one of hundreds all with the same level of talent, and ego will be very quick to notice the lack of attention from others around you in the class never mind the rejections that you will be dealing with.

You need to have explored every avenue of your decision completely before undertaking this road, including the possibility of an assessment by a professional trainer or at least attending acting classes to obtain an insight into your response. It may prove fruitful to attend several auditions and try out for a part prior to making decisions on your career direction, as once you commit to this particular field that is what most of your days will involve.

To be involved in the industry needs to be your primary goal in the beginning, obtaining work in the field of your preference to get you started whether it is movies, television, or even live theatre. So that you then have, the advantage to determine the type of work that appeals most in the event acting is not your true goal. You only need to read the credits at the end of a movie to see the opportunities available to be a part of that industry.

This will provide the best avenue to obtain the outcomes to reach that position of a complete life. Trusting your instinct is the key that will help open the doors to your future, yes there will be tough times and decisions. However, if you own the dream that is when the passion kicks in and your instinct and ego will want the goal to be successful.

Looking at another example, if when you were at school you loved art classes and had ideas of pursuing art as a career. However, due to your dislike of school overall, you quit and got a job. Secretly you never lost your love for art, still visiting art shows, galleries, know numerous artists works and always wanting to paint your own work.

You devise your plan to turn back the clock, complete your school education at night classes, after which you will then obtain an arts degree at college enabling you then to live the dream you lost by becoming a successful artist. The problem is; you are two months into attending night school and the realisation hits that you still hate school. Moreover, that there are no way you will last right through to obtaining a degree. The principle of "Stop, look and listen" will need applying at this point.

Stop, and reassess what it is you actually want to achieve. In the above example, it was to be able to paint your own work and presumably well enough to earn a living from it.

Look, at the plan you set out for yourself and determine what other options are available to reach your goal. In the above example, the first may have been to buy a set of paintbrushes, paints and canvas then actually attempt to paint something first to determine your responses. If you were excited, then your next step may be to attend private art classes. This is not about finding a short cut it is being realistic in what you know you can complete in pursuit of your dream.

This path will certainly help you realise what you do not know about painting techniques and more than likely, realise the need to complete the art classes before you complete that first painting.

Listen, to what your instinct is telling you. When the nerves are tingling, the hairs on your body are standing up; there are butterflies in the stomach to name a few indicators telling you that this is what you were born to do, especially if one or more occur when you realise you are near to completing your first painting.

Then of course, there are the various styles of art to consider if you already have a favourite well and good, if not then you will need to apply the "stop, look and listen" principle again to ensure you are choosing the right path. This is where your instinct will really come to the fore, for even though through the art classes you will be learning all the styles and categories of art. There will be one style in one category that will provide you with more pleasure, success and satisfaction than any of the rest.

Remaining dedicated, determined and persistent in whatever field you choose will ensure the day, when you will present your very own art show where your journey will then take you on a new path and life.

You can see from the art example of the pitfalls that are always present in any choice of career that you want to pursue. Do not jump to conclusions; thoroughly investigate all your opportunities. Test the waters wherever possible through volunteering, experimenting, part time work, etc. let ego do the talking, instinct do the walking, and you will know in your own heart as they say, exactly what path is yours.

Negative thoughts are a part of life that is how the ego works. Either you show that you are winning or ego assumes you are failing. Instinct needs to be constantly alert for those of you who are worrywarts or sensitive to criticism from others, real or perceived. Whenever the thought of doubt in your ability to cope appears Stop, challenge those thoughts. Look, at your plan and the achievements to this point, are you still on track, is the plan or timeframe still realistic. Listen, to why the doubts have surfaced.

The clue to finding the answer of whether your fears are only to justify the plan, or if you are in fact on the wrong path lies in the type of questions you ask yourself. The main question should be; "what am I actually struggling with". Which area of your life are you actually having difficulty with or accepting the challenge.

For instance, your current career may be coming more tedious as the excitement builds with each progressive step you make with your new adventure. It may only be your patience that is struggling, remind yourself constantly as to why you commenced this journey in the first place. The thoughts of your inability to cope will soon pass.

On the other hand, if there is that increasing feeling that your new adventure is not all you thought it would be, that you are wasting your time, you are not finding the field you are in as exciting or any such type of thoughts. You may in fact need to reassess the goal or field selection of the new career.

Another reason may be that your family is struggling to cope with the reduced attention you can give them. Resulting in feelings of guilt or selfishness on your part and you may need to revise the time schedule you have set yourself.

The support of your family is essential so providing them with as much information as you can, listening to their issues and being there when you can will help alleviate their concerns.

If you are struggling with your social life, unfortunately, this area suffers most during the transition period from the old career to the new, whether you are an outdoors or indoors person, this area of your life pays the price in the short term. This of course is the area that ego responds to the most, for you are imposing on the things that provide it with the most pleasure.

This is not to be confused with your personal time out; I have already said you need your own space away from work and family commitments and that it needs to be in your weekly and monthly plan.

If at some point, you made the decision to cut out your own personal time out spaces that you can better utilize that time in other areas. It could be a decision you will regret as it takes a unique type of character to live a life where there is no room for personal space or recreation.

These types of people are usually obsessed with their passion to succeed, often with a greed for power and/or money. They do not require any guidance in their quest, nor will family concerns come into the equation if it interferes with their quest.

I want to emphasize that even though some of your "fun time" may no longer be affordable in terms of time you have to spare, but your new project will provide in all probability much more enjoyment. The reality is that you need to make all areas (work, family, and social) as enjoyable as possible, this is what being positive is all about. Having that positive attitude enhances your energy, thus more focused and productive results are the enjoyable rewards. Remaining positive is one of the challenges you face, especially in a world where negativity is much more the norm.

The media constantly provides us with negative data from all over the globe, available 24/7 on the internet, on the hour on TV and radio programs, and reviewed daily in the newspapers. Providing as little time as possible if any, to this form of media information, you should view as a good thing unless journalism is your career path. Because mostly it is information, you are unable to do anything to change.

The less time you also have to spend around negative people the better, a very fruitful exercise will be to review the relationships that exist in all areas of your life. With a view of, reducing time-shared with negative people instead, drawing strength by forming relationships with the positive and energetic people who are of the same mindset that are now appearing in your life.

Maintaining a winning mindset and being persistent ensures that ego stays on track, the level of input you give determines the level of success you achieve and ego is the one that supplies that drive to succeed.

138

Keep in mind that the journey to achieving the goal is where you achieve the most satisfaction, because once you reach the end of this journey, it is human behaviour or should I say ego that will want more. The good news is this time you will be in a career that is satisfying, doing a job that you love.

CHAPTER 12

LIVING THE LIFE

There will be readers that will be at this page without having made a start to their journey, but if you have participated in the journey then for you this section will most likely be teaching the converted. For once, you have experienced your new life style you are not the same person that began this journey, having lived a life style that was for most purposes ego intelligence controlled. Instead, you now see life in a very different light.

Before I changed my life style I was very much an ego controlled person, I was also controlled by alcohol and nicotine, which only increased my ego thoughts about what was important to me and that I was having a "good time".

I do not want you to misunderstand, that person still exists there in my head, except the difference now is my ego-controlled thoughts have learnt to include instinct in those thoughts. Moreover, accepting those modified thoughts and acting in accordance with this new direction.

One of the most common observations you will face is the difficulties people have with a life controlled by ego and their continual search to be happy, constantly chasing the dream that if they only reach that next condition in life then they will be happy.

Whether it is the house, job, car, big TV, you name it their goal is never ending.

Their jubilance lasting only long enough until the next desire comes along particularly when related to material objects, and then they are unhappy because they no longer have the best available and they will not be happy until they have it.

The strange scenario is that often people who appear to have everything one could possibly want are still "not happy" attending psychologist therapy sessions in an attempt to find happiness. While for others, even though not having all of the comforts of life, are living in contentment satisfied with life.

By you having completed the journey I am confident you are now the person you were born to be and your life too is now in the latter group of the two just mentioned.

For as discussed being happy is merely a mood of the ego that can change from one moment to the next. Instead, by leading a life content with who you are and what you do required the combined effort of both the ego and the instinct.

This combined effort did not come easy, in a world that for the most part is ego controlled has required you to make many changes to your thinking methodology. Learning to accept that you are only responsible for your behaviour and having to accept that you are not responsible for the behaviour of all those in your life requires plenty of fortitude.

It is very difficult to observe someone that is close to you and excessively controlled by his or her ego, you feel you need to say something but know it would be futile knowing what it has taken you to make the change.

Another interesting observation I have made is questioning ego-controlled adults on the age they feel they are. Very rarely have I come across a person, who accepts their age, in fact they generally claim to feel 10-15 years less than their age providing they be in reasonable health. This phenomenon gains more importance when you consider the numbers of injuries occurring to people who overrule their instinct to participate in activities that their body is not in any condition to perform.

Occasionally you will meet people that appear interested in why you are you as long as it is the short version, but you are no longer offended when they cut you off to divert the subject back to them.

You will discover that you are more of a listener now than you were, it is not necessary anymore to get your opinion heard on the topics that people around you are having. In fact, there will be times where you will observe someone expressing his or her opinion so strongly that you will not find the need to disagree though you do; you know that in their mind only their opinions are the right ones.

When people discover you are a good listener you will hear more of the emotional issues happening in their lives than before. They will not want you to solve their problems nor should you try, all they need is someone to listen to their latest issue that is making them unhappy. Often wanting agreement with their side of the story is all the help they are requiring, it is best in this situation if you listen to your instinct before you speak, if at all.

Another discovery waiting for you is that because instinct is playing a major part in your thoughts now, you will express more emotion, having feelings regarding many situations that before this journey you would not have given the time of day for.

Not ego type emotion as with positive and negative thoughts, but more of caring or loving thoughts especially family, and for men the saying that grown men do not cry is no longer applicable.

Tears that flow from an ego-controlled mind are usually the result of disappointment when failing or over-zealous when successful; the tears I am referring to here are often because of someone else's joy or grief.

You now are able to feel their joy or pain, these are feelings you must not try to repress, as that will affect your well-being. There is no reason to feel embarrassed about crying when it comes from the heart, for men or for women as it is a natural expression of the instinct.

The other areas you will now have emotive feelings for are the animals and the environment. I know for myself that there was a time when I enjoyed hunting, however these days I struggle to eliminate any living creature even a mosquito that has just bitten me.

There was also a time when if the grass or plants were dying from lack of water that meant no mowing or trimming, now days I still do not enjoy mowing or trimming but I will spare as much water as allowed to ensure their survival.

I mentioned a moment ago that my ego of yesteryear was still a part of me today that is why this new path requires constant review between the two intelligence systems.

The ego that you developed during your formative years and over your pre, instinct awareness years will always be a part of your thinking style, however, the difference now is that your reasoning capabilities provide a far better outcome for you and for those in your life.

You will need to make regular checks on all of your decisions, that it is a dual one and you have not slipped back into letting ego control your thoughts for it will.

Ego is cunning you need to be mindful that it will have a conversation with itself in an endeavor to choose the best form of attack for a winning result. Engaging in role-play is an ego characteristic that is identifiable by recognising the outcome trying to be achieved, generally one that will only excite the ego.

The ego and instinct issues you identified through the journey that related to your personality or any of the other negative behaviour conditions that were prevalent in your life, to know that they no longer are an influence in your life today needs regular reviews put on your life plan as well.

One area that will require practice is acting upon your intuitive thoughts, in the beginning it may seem hit and miss with some results however, continued practice produces satisfying results that you are now aware in comparison to before when you thought it was fate or luck.

Constant awareness of the virtues in your character is a good subject to have between ego and instinct for regular communication during idle moments and some examples that you could keep on your mind are:

> TLC—Tenderness, Loving, Caring toward your family and friends.
>
> RRR—Responsible, Reliable, Respectful toward your work colleagues and work habits
>
> TTT—Truthful, Trustworthy, Tolerant toward everyone including yourself.
>
> CCC—Courteous, considerate, compassionate toward those less fortunate than yourself.

These and other acronyms that you may prefer to create that will help ego to remember not only the words but also their functions.

Maintaining the daily routine of looking and listening whether through walking, running or riding amongst natural beauties in order to ensure ego remains a good listener is an essential part of your ritual or maintenance plan.

Healthy eating habits and daily exercise should now be fitting into your life plan and only you need to know that you are practicing looking and listening techniques.

Included in that daily routine will need to be at least one session of meditation for this is the opportunity for the instinct to experience complete absence of thought without the chatter of the ego.

Having regular checkups with your local G.P. and dentist is a compulsory addition to your life plan, as is performing regular checks on yourself to keep you aware of any changes to your body.

Next to looking after yourself, it is also required of you to look after your family so including them in your health and exercise activities will do them no harm, or at least encouraging them to participate.

One last thing, there is a saying "You work to live not live to work" if you have that new career or even in the same career, ensure that you do not let your work life take control of your life. Do not let ego believe that it is irreplaceable, for it will do.

Most of all enjoy the life that you have received, try not to take it too seriously for as I said some time ago now, you are only here for a miniscule amount of time and it is up to you to make that life as fruitful as possible.

You and only you now have the skills and ability to achieve that enjoyment if you have put in the work I have given you throughout the book, which I am sure is now the life you are living.

THE CLOSING

At the beginning of our journey together, I said you would recognise three key areas to improve your life. This is something that only you can answer, but I am confident that by completing this book you will have achieved those key points.

The reward itself is you now know your behaviour patterns and how to live your life controlling them, and if you have taken the opportunity to be living your work life doing what you love doing then you can ask no more from the life you were given.

The person you were born to be is the person that is welcome in any society. Therefore, by you living the life that encompasses all the virtues of your instinct, ensures you are welcome wherever you go.

I hope this book has provided you the opportunity to make improvements to your life regardless whether they were big or small, particularly if you are now able to include more of the standards of instinct to your behaviour each day.

I would especially like to thank you for the opportunity of including me to be a part of the journey through your life. More significantly if I was able to help change any areas of your life that are now providing you with a better personal life to that prior to us meeting, that you will stay on this path as you continue your journey through life, above all else, to enjoy your time on this earth.